A WORLD WITHIN

GEORGE WEBBER
2007

A WORLD WITHIN

AN INTIMATE PORTRAIT OF THE LITTLE BOW HUTTERITE COLONY

Text and Photographs by George Webber

With a Foreword by David J. Goa

FIFTH HOUSE

Fifth House Ltd. edition first published in 2005

Cover and interior photographs by George Webber
Cover and interior design by Kathy Aldous-Schleindl
Edited/copyedited by Geri Rowlatt
Proofread by Ann Sullivan
Scans by St. Solo Computer Graphics

The publisher gratefully acknowledges the support of The Canada Council for the Arts and the Department of Canadian Heritage.

Canada Council for the Arts | Conseil des Arts du Canada

We acknowledge the financial support of the Government of Canada through the Book Publishing Industry Development Program for our publishing activities.

Printed in Canada by Friesens

05 06 07 08 09/ 5 4 3 2 1

First published in the United States in 2005 by
Fitzhenry & Whiteside
121 Harvard Avenue, Suite 2
Allston, MA 02134

Library and Archives Canada Cataloguing in Publication

Webber, George, 1952-
A world within : an intimate portrait of the Little Bow Hutterite Colony / George Webber. — 1st ed.

ISBN 1-894856-60-0
1. Little Bow Hutterite Colony—Pictorial works. 2. Hutterian Brethren—Alberta—Little Bow River Region—Pictorial works.
I. Title.

BX8129.H8W42 2005 289.7'71234
C2004-906447-9

Fifth House Ltd.
A Fitzhenry & Whiteside Company
1511, 1800-4 St. SW
Calgary, Alberta T2S 2S5

1-800-387-9776
www.fitzhenry.ca

CONTENTS

TO REALIZE THE KINGDOM OF GOD

DAVID J. GOA

This is a book born of spiritual friendship. George Webber invites us to glimpse, as he did, the lives and sensibilities of the children, women, and men of the Little Bow Hutterite Colony, an hour south of Calgary. Webber took the first photographs on Easter Sunday, 1999, and the last on Easter Sunday, 2003.

The Little Bow Colony was built in the beautiful Little Bow River valley, straddling the river and protected from the winds that sweep off the Rocky Mountains. On the west side of the river were the living quarters, hog barn, poultry houses, kindergarten, kitchen, and slaughterhouse. On the east side were the remaining farm buildings for the storage and maintenance of agricultural machinery, along with the cattle and dairy barns. The colony was located twenty kilometres west of Champion.

Long-term water management planning by the Government of Alberta called for a dam on the Little Bow, two kilometres downstream from where it flowed through the colony. That dam would service the irrigation district to the south. In 1999 Webber learned that the colony would have to move and that the dam would form a lake that would put the Little Bow Colony under thirty metres of water. The colony and the government arranged a land swap, which includes new building stock for the Brethren located within reasonable reach of their agricultural land on higher ground away from the river.

The story leading to this book began in the late 1980s when Webber became interested in the plain people of the Prairies and began his pilgrimages of exploration that eventually included visits and friendships with more than twenty colonies sprinkled over the landscape of Alberta and Saskatchewan. Many of us who grew up on the

Prairies have seen Hutterite colonies from the highways and taken a second glance at the children, women, and men in plain clothing when we pass them on the streets of Athabasca, Camrose, Red Deer, and Lethbridge or when we encounter them in the markets and hospitals of Edmonton and Calgary. Periodically, we read about them in the newspapers, usually when there is a local dispute over development of a new colony. The reasons local farmers give for not wanting to have Hutterian Brethren as neighbours are often remarkably similar to those used in the fifteenth century, when the community was formed in the lowlands of Europe, in the early twentieth century, when the whole of the community was forced to migrate from Russia to the United States in the face of the emerging Soviet Union, and following the First World War, when persecution forced them to move to Western Canada.

Despite all this, the Hutterian Brethren are the most successful communal movement in the history of Western Europe, and they have flourished in Canada. Many of the District Agriculturalists with whom I have talked over the years say, without hesitation, that they are the first farmers to seek new information on agricultural practice and to make use of the latest technology and that they are among the most efficient and productive of the farmers who have developed the agricultural base of Western Canada. Their large workforce and communal way of life make them self-sufficient, and they do not suffer unduly from either whimsical weather or unstable markets. Even during the intense seasons of planting and harvest, when their independent neighbours work alone from sun-up to after sunset, the Brethren's pattern of shared work leaves them with noticeably less pressure and more confidence. Neighbours notice such things and, I suspect, this is one source of the local uneasiness that occasionally arises when word gets out of plans for a new colony. In the census for 2001, Alberta had 26,300 Hutterian Brethren, up 22 percent from 1991. The median age is twenty-two and the most recent statistics show 295 colonies in Canada, of which 140 were in Alberta, 95 in Manitoba, and 55 in Saskatchewan. An additional five colonies fall in the metropolitan statistical records of Statistics Canada. The Hutterian Brethren have become an integral part of Alberta's textured cultural landscape.

There is, of course, another source for the concern and anxiety that have been publicly expressed since the Brethren immigrated en masse to Canada in 1918. The Hutterian Brethren embody their difference and live out the genius of their faith. It shapes their common life, presentation, and participation in the life of the world. While many greet this difference with fear, Webber, who also lives out his Christian faith rooted in the Roman Catholic tradition, welcomed it as an opportunity for friendship in the hope it would both open up avenues for his understanding of the Hutterian faith and life and deepen his spiritual life in the face-to-face meeting. Indeed, this is what we see in and through his photographic study. It is a witness to Webber's presence in and among the Hutterian Brethren and his regard for them and their presence as citizens of Canada. Webber, through this study, and the Hutterian Brethren, through opening their life and understanding to him, have taken another step along that path most treasured by the Brethren: the realization of the Kingdom of God, found first and foremost in mutual regard free of fear.

The children, women, and men of the Little Bow Hutterian Brethren Colony existed because of the vitality of "the living faith of the dead." This story unfolds on two continents over more than five hundred years. It is a story that has shaped their sense of purpose and their life.

THE TERROR OF HISTORY

The Hutterian Brethren are a branch of the Anabaptist movement that emerged during the Reformation. This tradition of religious thinking and life played a substantial role in the development of humanism, ushered in a new critique of state-sponsored religion, contributed to the development of doctrines on separation of church and state, and provided a theological alternative to the religious arguments for holy crusades and the theory of just war. Their doctrine and discipline of "yieldedness" suggested there was no foundation in the Gospels of Jesus Christ for killing another human being. All human beings—heretic, infidel, sinner, and saint—were created in the "image and likeness of God," and Christians are called by faith to "yield" their own life instead of engaging in violence. It is a demanding ethical teaching, and the various Brethren communities that formed around it saw sharing "all things in common" as providing the kind of community context that made it possible to fulfill their divine obligation.

The Hutterian wing of the Anabaptist family was organized by Jacob Hutter (d.1536), a Swiss hat maker and one of the early ministers within this communion. He promulgated the practice of believer's baptism through which adults might willingly turn away from the life and impulses of self-fulfillment in the world and towards the kingdom of God and a life of service. His early preaching on the biblical prohibition against taking oaths and on yieldedness (including pacifism and resisting military service) led the community into immediate conflict with the emerging nations of Europe. Hutter also taught that the community was to remain a "separate people," unassimilated into the regular pattern of community life. The Hutterian Brethren claim 1528 as the date of their founding because it was then that Hutter and the other elders of the community called upon them to pool their resources—unlike their Anabaptist counterparts, the Amish and the Mennonites.

Hutter, a superb organizer, began giving shape to many of the disparate Anabaptist communities in

Switzerland and Moravia. In 1529 he travelled from Tyrol to Moravia, preaching the need to "realize the Kingdom of God" through a shared life, separation from the world, and yieldedness. He brought many communities under his new organizational umbrella. During one of his journeys to Moravia, in 1536, he was abducted, imprisoned, and tortured. He refused to give up his beliefs on the separation of church and state, the taking of oaths, and pacifism. He argued that the type of economic communalism that they had formed with their fledgling communities was the result of a clear command of the Gospel, reflected the shape of the early church in Jerusalem, and was imperative for the realization of the Kingdom of God. His teaching and effectiveness in organizing and inspiring many people so incensed the authorities that in February of that year, three years into his leadership, he was burned at the stake, thus becoming one of the first generation of martyrs through whose blood "the seeds of faith were planted" in European soil.

Hutter's leadership passed to Hans Amon, but his untimely death in 1542 brought Hutter's former assistant, Peter Riedeman, to the fore. He continued building the foundations of the communities of the common life and set in motion what came to be known as the "golden period" of the Brethren. Riedeman was imprisoned for nine years and died in 1556. Over the next half-century, the community grew to approximately twenty-five thousand members.

The "golden period" of the Brethren came to an end in 1599 with the advent of the Counter-Reformation. The series of persecutions over the next two hundred years created new generations of martyrs. By 1622 most of the property of the various communities had been confiscated and many of the Brethren had fled to Slovakia and Transylvania, where they were re-established under the leadership of Andrew Ehrenpreis (d.1662). In Slovakia they soon came face-to-face with the invading Turks. In the late eighteenth century many were forced into "external conversion" to Roman Catholicism. Despite this, the Brethren maintained a form of co-operative living and, in secret, maintained elements of their religious and organizational structure. In Transylvania the resettlement of a substantial German Lutheran population changed the political and cultural landscape, which allowed the Brethren to restore their moribund colony in the 1750s. It lasted for only a few years and, in 1767, they were forced to flee again, first to Wallachia and then, welcomed by Catherine the Great, into the region of Ukraine. When the German princess Sophie Friederike Auguste von Anhalt-Zerbst (1729–96) became Empress of Russia in 1762, she insisted on bringing German-speaking peoples into the empire to aid in its development. Many Anabaptists, including the Hutterian Brethren, saw this as an opportunity to escape the persecutions in Western Europe and accepted her invitation to resettle.

Catherine the Great promised religious freedom to the Brethren and in return extracted a commitment from them not to engage in the evangelization of their Russian neighbours. This promise remained intact until 1870, when it was withdrawn and the Brethren, along with their spiritual cousins the Mennonites, became subject to conscription. Thus, the North American chapter in Anabaptist history opened in 1874 with immigration to both the United States and Canada, a process that continued into the early years of Communist rule in the Soviet Union. The Hutterian Brethren were among the first to make the decision to migrate. Between 1874 and 1877 the entire Hutterite population, more than one thousand members, immigrated to the United States. Of this group, approximately four hundred had remained faithful to "holding all things common" and they established three separate colonies (*Bruderhofs*) in South Dakota.

All of the North American Hutterian communities trace their origins to one of the three original colonies that came in the 1870s. These mother colonies were named for the person who was head of the colony at the time of migration. The *Dariusleut* (Darius people) arrived in 1874 under the leadership of Darius Walter. In 1877 the *Schmiedeleut* (Blacksmith people) of Michael Waldner, a blacksmith, followed. The *Lehrerleut* (Teacher people), led by Jacob Wipf, a teacher, arrived in South Dakota in 1879. This latter group did not practise the community of goods in Russia, but many of them took up the practice in South Dakota. Each of the communities in Canada identifies with one of these original communities. The Little Bow colony is *Dariusleut*.

At the outbreak of the First World War, when the issue of conscription again arose, there were seventeen hundred adults ("souls") living on seventeen *Bruderhofs*. The Anabaptist teaching of yieldedness remained strong in the South Dakota Brethren communities so they refused to participate in the war effort. Since the First World War pitted the Allies against Germany, and since the Hutterian Brethren were a German-speaking people, the local population in South Dakota took great exception to their refusal to serve. A number of Brethren were imprisoned during the war because they were conscientious objectors. They were treated severely in federal prisons and one died during this ordeal. Both the pressure of the Local State Council of Defense and the hostility of the local community led to the migration of sixteen of the seventeen *Bruderhofs* to Canada in 1918, immediately following the war. In both Canada and the United States, the Brethren were granted conscientious objector status in the Second World War.

SPIRITUAL LIFE TO "REALIZE THE KINGDOM OF GOD"

The spiritual life of the Hutterian Brethren has its roots in the formative events of the Swiss Brethren movement in Zurich (1484–1511), under the leadership of Conrad Grebel (1498–1526). Grebel, a son of one of Zurich's leading families, was educated at the Universities of Basel, Vienna, and Paris, where he was steeped in the new humanism that swept through the intellectual life of Europe. He experienced a profound religious renewal in 1522 under the teaching of Ulrich Zwingli (1484–1531), one of the foremost fathers of the Reformation, and became his friend and supporter. In the heat of the theological and institutional debates that characterized the Reformation, Zwingli decided to develop a state-church type of reformation, which led Grebel to part company from him from 1523 to 1525. Grebel then became the leader of a small group, located largely in Zurich and the nearby village of Zollikon. Grebel and his followers taught that the New Testament called for a church of intentional believers, a church separate from the state, and that the true church was inaugurated through adult baptism. His group evangelized with vigour and rapidly grew in Zurich and the surrounding cantons. Grebel was imprisoned in Zurich in October 1525 as a propagator of a proscribed faith. He escaped in April 1526 and wandered as an itinerant evangelist until he died of plague in August of that year.

Grebel developed a set of foundational ideas that came to shape many Anabaptist movements, including the Hutterian Brethren. Christianity, he argued, is essentially a form of discipleship (*Nachfolge Christi*), requiring a new birth that actually transforms one's way of thinking and one's life. Instead of living according to personal ambition and the aspirations of civil society, one must pattern one's life after Jesus Christ and his teachings. That second idea laid the foundation both for the critique of all state churches and for the Hutterian understanding of the colony as a form of church. That is, church is a free association, not a matter of birthright or citizenship. It is a brotherhood of adults who have voluntarily made the commitment to follow Christ and have separated themselves from the ideals, values, and sensibilities of the world to live in holiness. It is the fruit of holiness, the pattern of Christ's life and teaching, that provided the third idea. An ethic of love must govern all one's decisions and relationships. This ethic, which trumps the obligation of citizens to serve in defence of the nation, is a radical form of Christian pacifism, arguing that all forms of violence and support of violence are contrary to the Gospel of Jesus Christ. Grebel died before these ideas could be fully developed, and it was left to his followers, including the Hutterian Brethren, to give shape and form to a life that showed their compelling value.

The Hutterian Brethren affirm the central teachings shared by virtually all of the Christian traditions since they were given form in the Nicene Creed in 325. They affirm the doctrine of the Trinity and the divinity of Jesus of Nazareth. What is perhaps most distinctive is their understanding of the church and the shape and form discipleship takes for those who are baptized as a matter of willed decision into communion with it. The Christian faith requires one to overcome personal ambition and reject the amusements commonly found in the world. In a document published in 1965 and broadly circulated through various Hutterite communities, the Brethren speak of a current set of these amusements, including "the dance, the theater, the card-party, carousals, the pool-room, smoking, the circus, the motion-picture show, television and radios in the homes, the popular bathing resorts," and any social gathering where it is not possible to glorify God (*The Hutterian Brethren of Montana*, Augusta, MT: Hutterian Brethren of Montana, 1965).

The mission of Christianity is to reform and convert the unregenerate world and to realize the Kingdom of God on earth through a pattern of life where personal ambition is transformed into a life of loving communion. The colony, where all things are held in common, models this surrender and provides a context in which each person may grow in the love of others through participating in the household of faith. The purpose of the colony is cultivation of holiness, and it is only through such a life that one has the capacity to resist the normal obligations of citizenship and live committed to the ethic of love. The experience of centuries of persecution joins with Hutterian theological teaching to make a compelling case for their opposition to war. They entirely reject military service. Service during wartime under civil organizations, when organizations such as the YMCA or Red Cross are temporarily allied with the military, is prohibited, as is participation in any way in the financing of war operations, including the purchase of war bonds and the payment of war taxes. Support for civilian relief efforts because of war, however, has been one of the areas where Hutterites have joined their Mennonite cousins and participated in various aid projects.

There is a deep consistency in their relationship to the state. Each colony builds and maintains its own elementary school, fulfilling the legal obligation to send children to school until they are fifteen. During peacetime they do not hesitate to pay property, corporate, and income taxes as required. Their desire to be free of state obligations that may be contrary to their values has meant they do not vote in elections or accept pensions or state social security benefits. They are quite capable of caring for their own as a part of the Gospel of love, and this responsibility should, under no circumstances, be surrendered to the state.

The Hutterian Brethren, whether the initial communities that gathered around Jacob Hutter or the Little Bow Colony that is the subject of George Webber's photographic study, are modelled on the early church founded in Jerusalem. The account of this early community of the "people of the way," as the followers of Jesus called themselves, is found in the book of Acts of the Apostles in the New Testament. It remains perhaps the most remarkable account in all of ancient literature of institutional formation and order. The account, attributed to the Apostle Luke, opens with the formation of the church at Pentecost in those heated days when the fledgling persecuted community of disciples was sorting out the implications of their newfound faith: "And fear came upon every soul: and many wonders and signs were done by the apostles. And all that believed were together, and had all things common; and sold their possessions and goods, and parted them to all men, as every man had need" (Acts 2:44–45). The first act of the Jerusalem community upon receiving the Holy Spirit was to join together in a dependent community of goods.

For the Jerusalem community almost two thousand years ago, the commitment to the Gospel of love prompted them to risk a life dependent on their brothers and sisters in their hope of realizing the Kingdom of God. As it was for the Jerusalem church, so it is for the Hutterian Brethren. The community of goods is a pathway to the realization of the Kingdom of God. Jerusalem is present in the life of the Little Bow Colony. We are invited to glimpse it through the skill and eye of George Webber, because he, like his Brethren friends, held spiritual friendship to be the heart of life.

SUGGESTED READINGS

Bennett, John William. *Hutterian Brethren: The Agricultural Economy and Social Organization of a Communal People.* Stanford, CA: Stanford University Press, 1967.

———. "Social Theory and the Social Order of the Hutterian Community." *The Mennonite Quarterly Review*, 51 (1977): 292–307.

Gross, Leonard. *The Golden Years of the Hutterites: The Witness and Thought of the Communal Moravian Anabaptists during the Walpot Era, 1565–1578.* Studies in Anabaptist and Mennonite History, no. 23. Scottsdale, PA: Herald Press, 1980.

Hostetler, John Andrew. *Hutterite Society*. Baltimore, MD: Johns Hopkins University Press, 1974.

Peters, Victor. *All Things Common: The Hutterian Way of Life.* Minneapolis, MN: University of Minnesota Press, 1965.

THE LITTLE BOW HUTTERITE COLONY

GEORGE WEBBER

Life on Southern Alberta's Little Bow Hutterite Colony is much like that on the nearly three hundred Hutterite colonies that dot the landscape of Western Canada. The Hutterites believe that the essential values of their faith will be preserved best in the rural isolation of their communities, which typically number from eighty-five to one hundred individuals.

In the late 1990s the people of Little Bow Colony were told that they would have to move. A major dam and water diversion project would eventually see the place where their houses and barns and church stood submerged under thirty metres of water.

After hearing this, I made a trip to the colony on Easter Sunday 1999. Would I be able to enter into this closed and very private community with my camera, or would this story forever go untold?

It took time to get the necessary permissions and win the trust of the community. I started slowly, initially photographing only the buildings and animals of the colony and returning each time with a gift of prints. After several months I became a familiar and welcomed visitor and, eventually, a friend to the people of Little Bow. I was welcomed into the barns, the gardens, the kitchen, the school, the dining room, and ultimately into the church. Working with a small, quiet rangefinder camera, I sought to be a gentle, unobtrusive witness to what I saw.

Over the course of four years, I witnessed the daily life and, finally, the abandonment of life on the colony in the spring of 2002.

Those of us who work in the documentary tradition find special meaning in recording those stories and events for which we feel a strong personal and spiritual connection. The camera is a tool that affirms and connects us to life.

I look to this passage from John for encouragement and inspiration in my work:

> *He came as a witness,*
> *as a witness to speak for the light,*
> *so that everyone might believe through him.*
>
> (John 1, 6–7)

The Hutterites lead lives of great spirituality, simplicity, and self-discipline. To spend time among them is to be reminded of the value of those things and to be touched by the continuing vitality of their 450-year-old faith tradition.

On Easter Sunday 2003, I returned to the colony site. It was exactly four years since my first visit to Little Bow Colony. A broad, shallow lake now covered all that had been. The walls of the valley shimmered in the dwindling light. The flat mirror surface of the water reflected the pale sky.

As I stood looking down, I was struck by the great beauty of the valley and by the impermanence of what had been.

The people of Little Bow had moved on to start a new life.

LITTLE BOW HUTTERITE COLONY JOURNAL

EASTER SUNDAY 1999

I drive onto the colony site and turn my truck off. Paul Hofer approaches. I introduce myself and tell him of my wish to photograph the colony. Paul is friendly but tells me that I will have to speak to the colony boss and minister for permission and they are not available to see me now. I ask if I might be able to walk around the colony perimeter and take some pictures. He tells me that will be all right. He introduces me to his son Steve, who is about twenty years old. Steve walks with me and takes me to see a series of teepee rings just south of the main colony site.

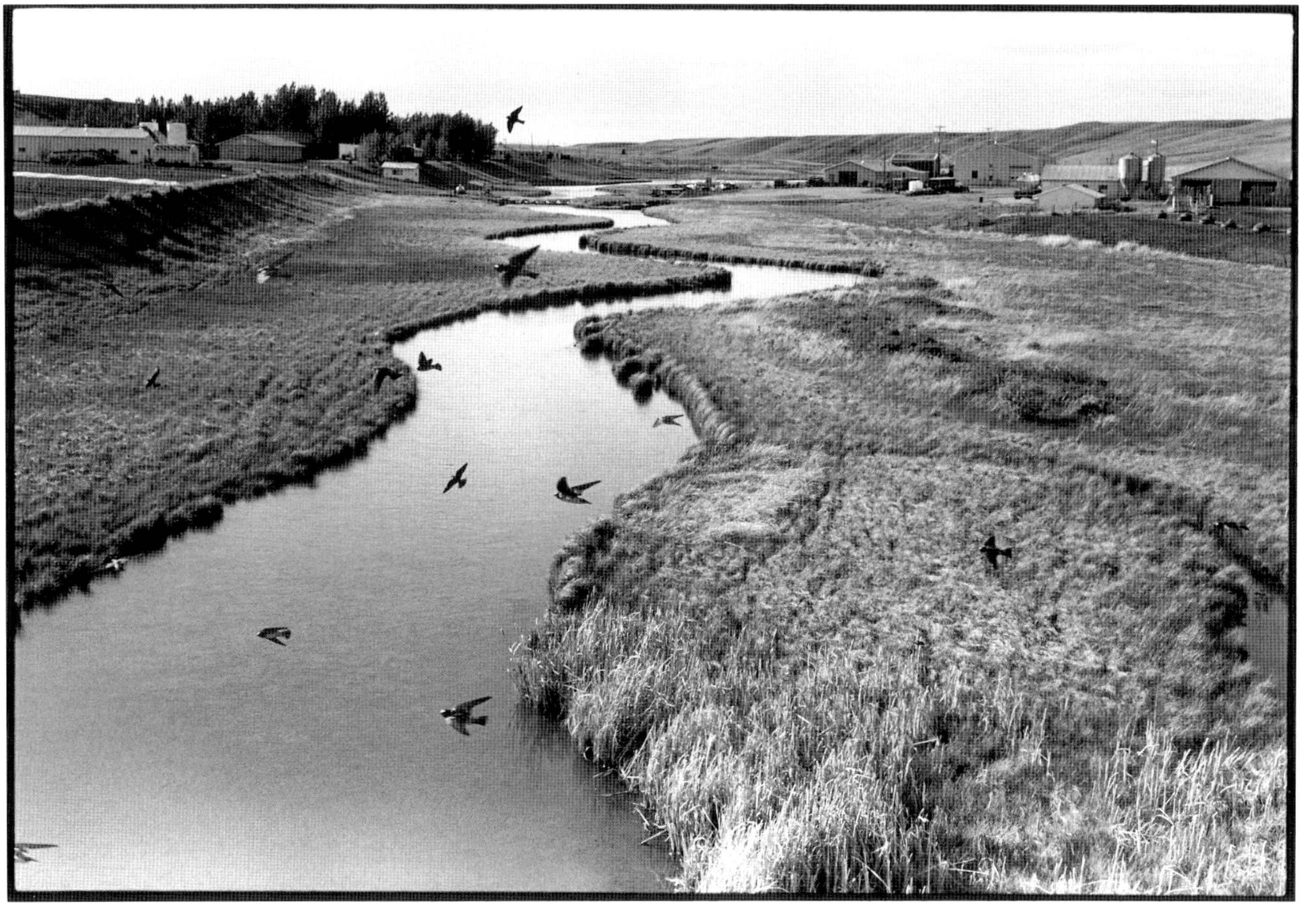

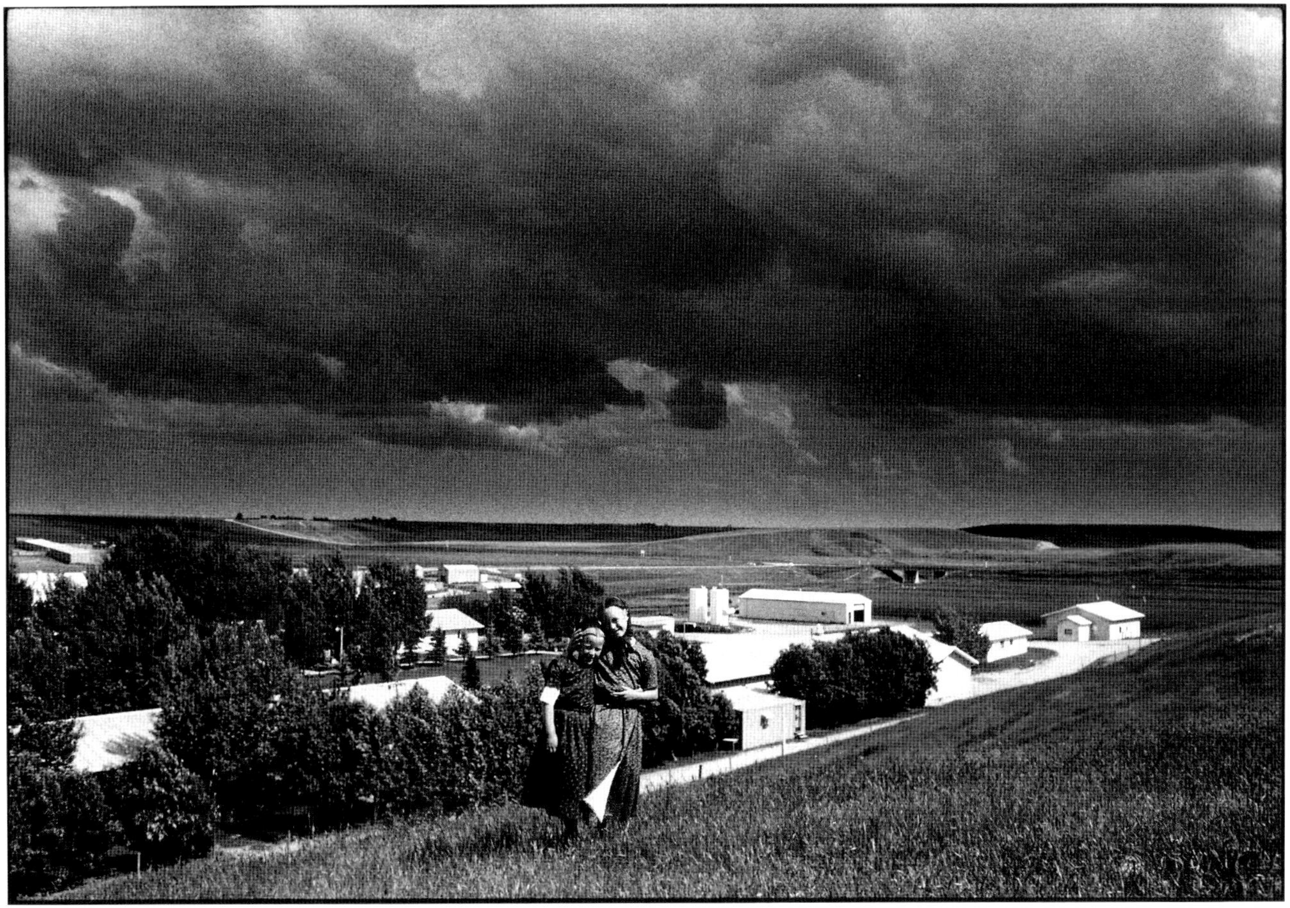

TOWARDS THE KINGDOM OF GOD

JUNE 5, 1999

Children sit around the big rock above the colony singing for me, mainly country and western ballads with beautiful harmonies. As I close my eyes and listen, I'm reminded of what Paul Gauguin said, "I shut my eyes in order to see."

NOVEMBER 1999

Little Maria sprints across the field to hand me half of a golden apple. She happily munches away on the other half .... a golden apple under a blue-black sky.

AUGUST 24, 2001

Helped harvesting corn and tomatoes. Dinner with children outside—hot dogs, slices of fresh cucumber, and corn on the cob we had picked earlier that day ... sitting on the lawn surrounded by the kids ... the girls keep bringing me more and more corn and ice tea. *God*, would I love to have a picture of this ... as close to heaven as I am likely to get on this earth.

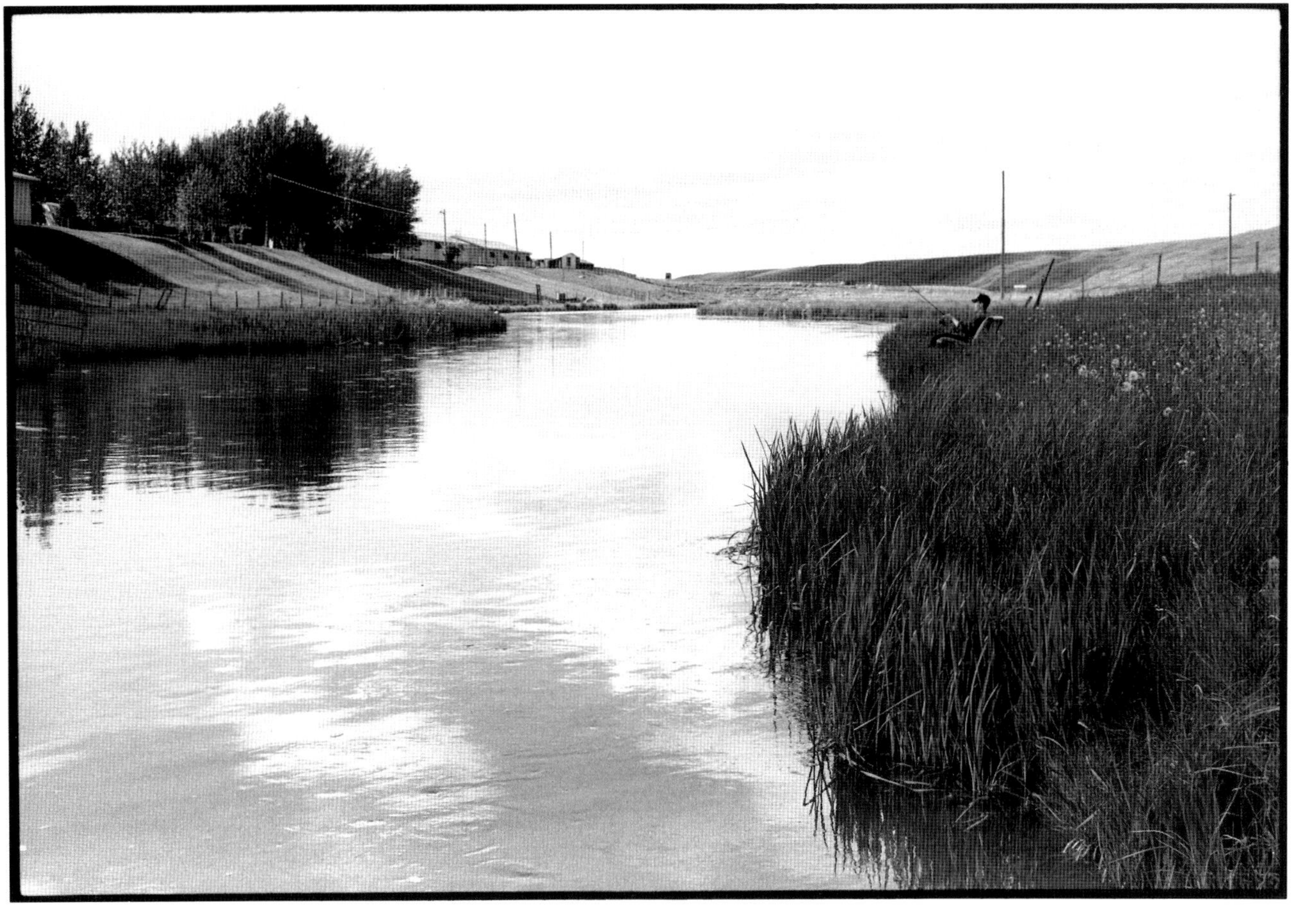

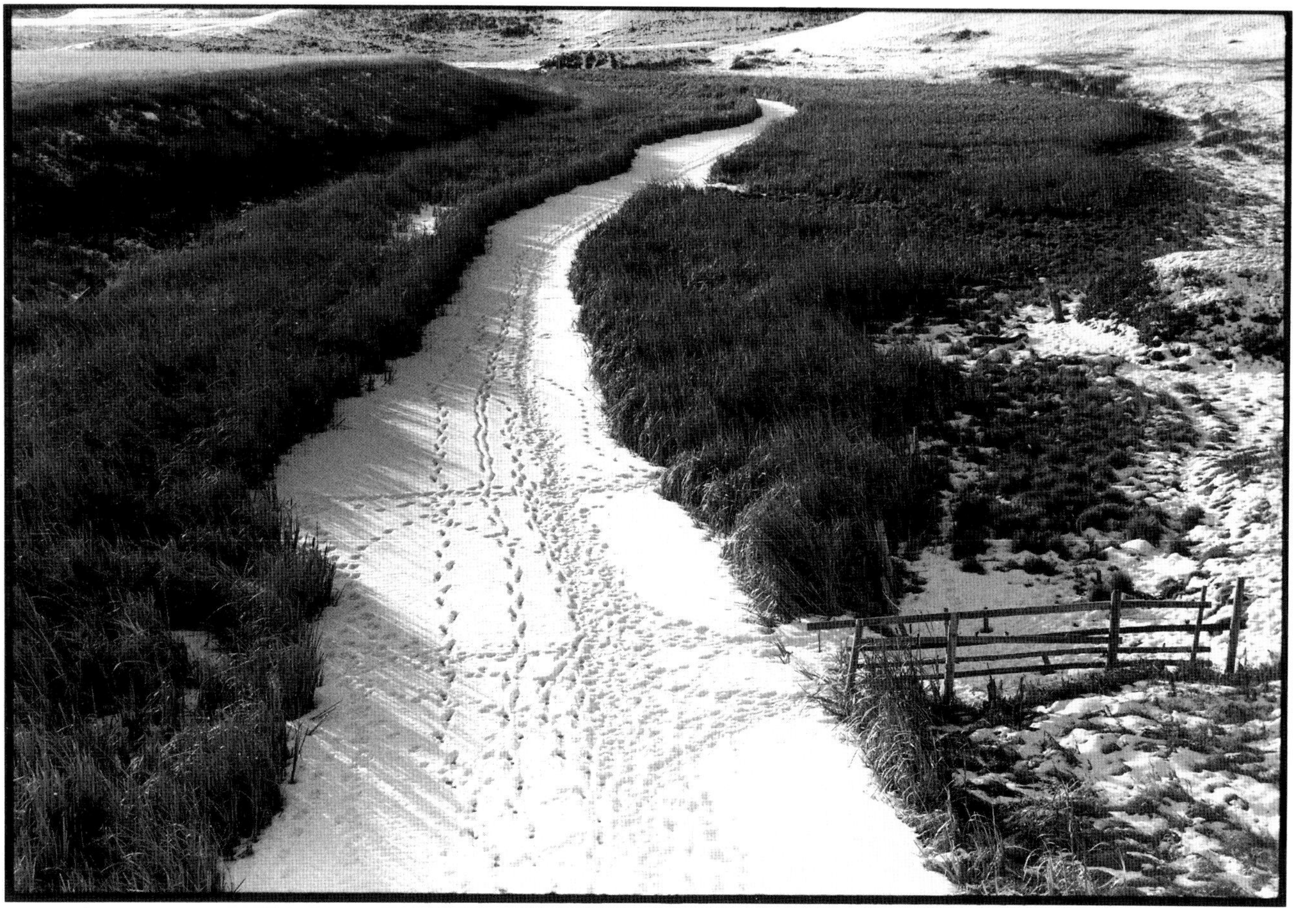

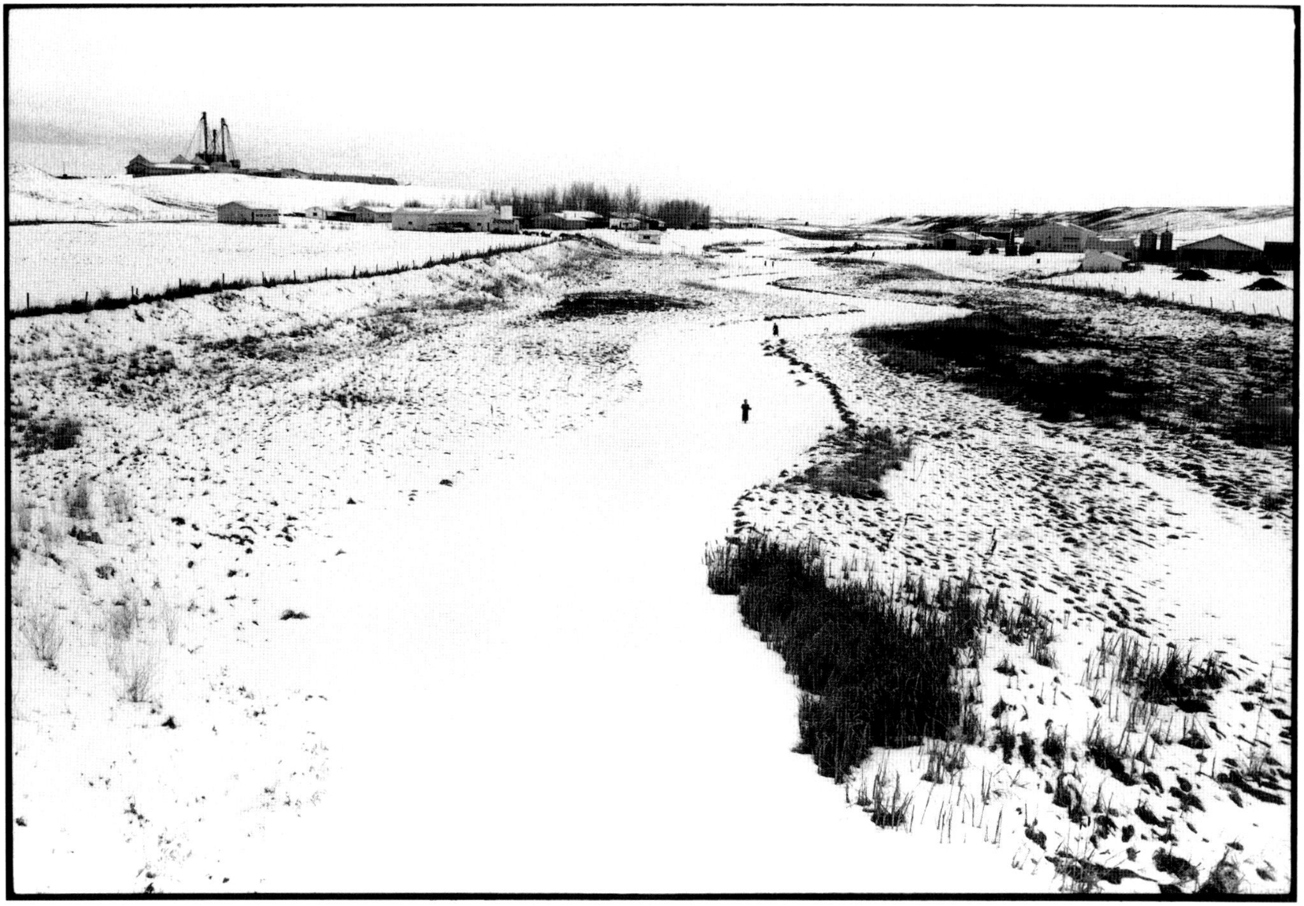

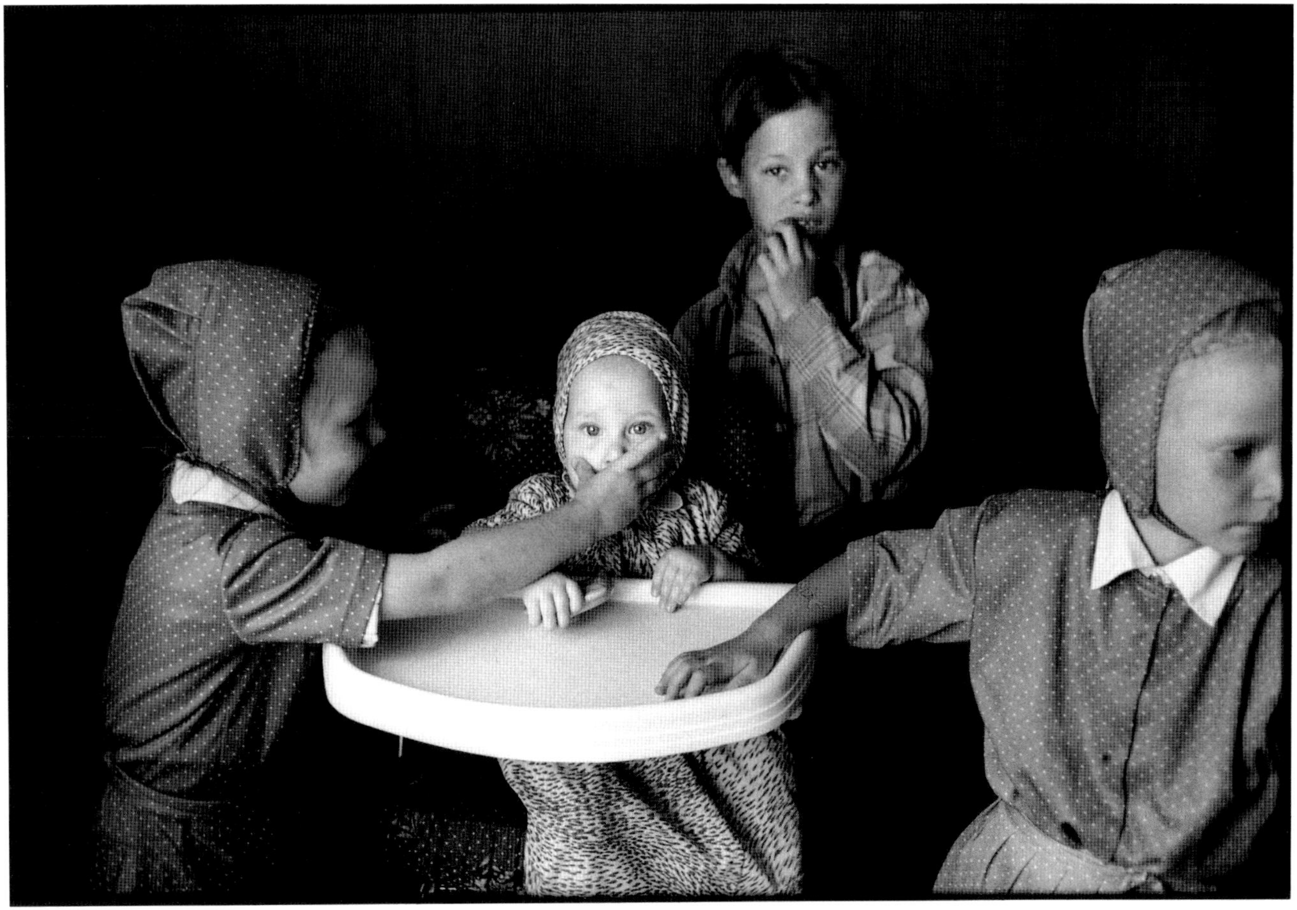

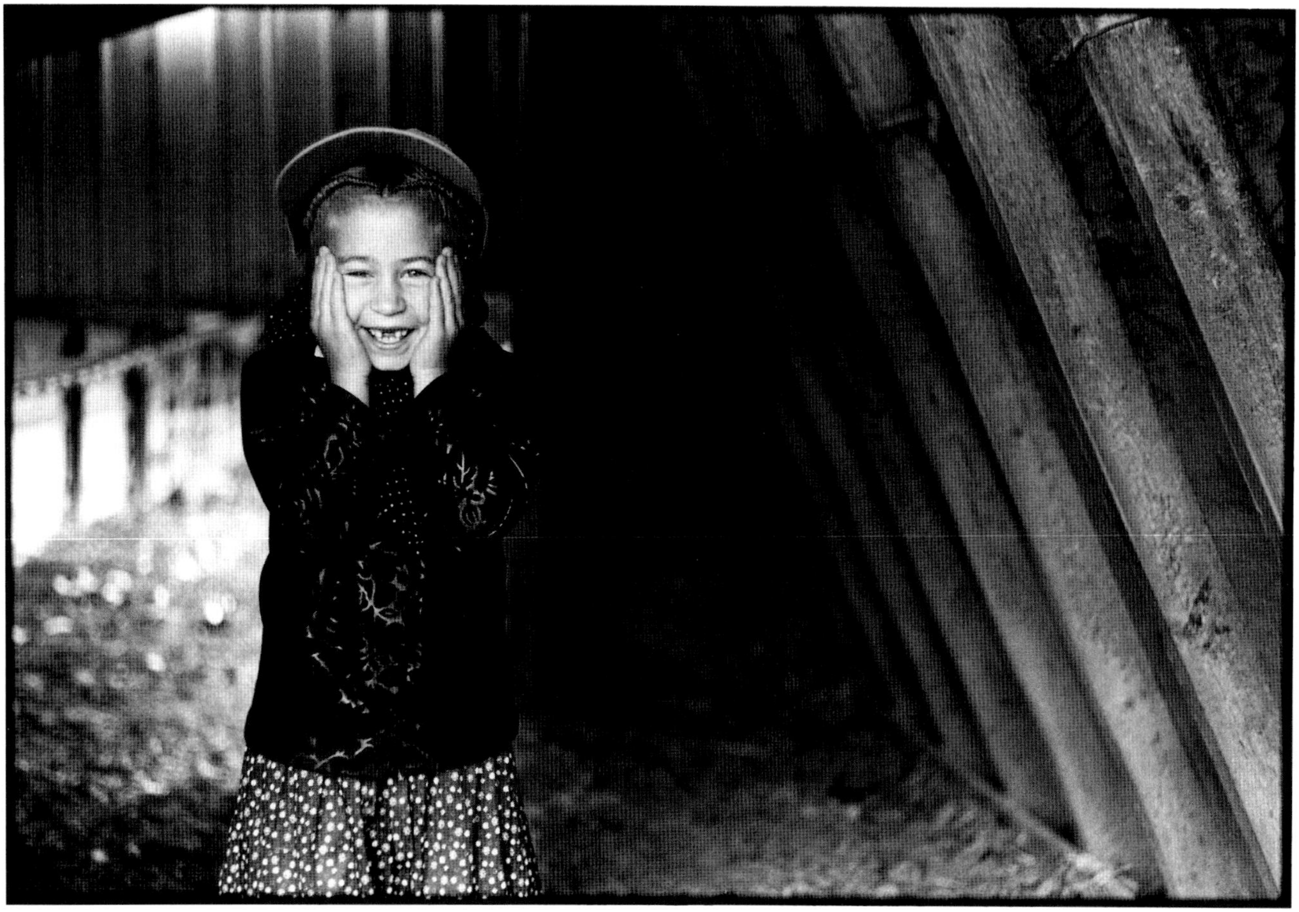

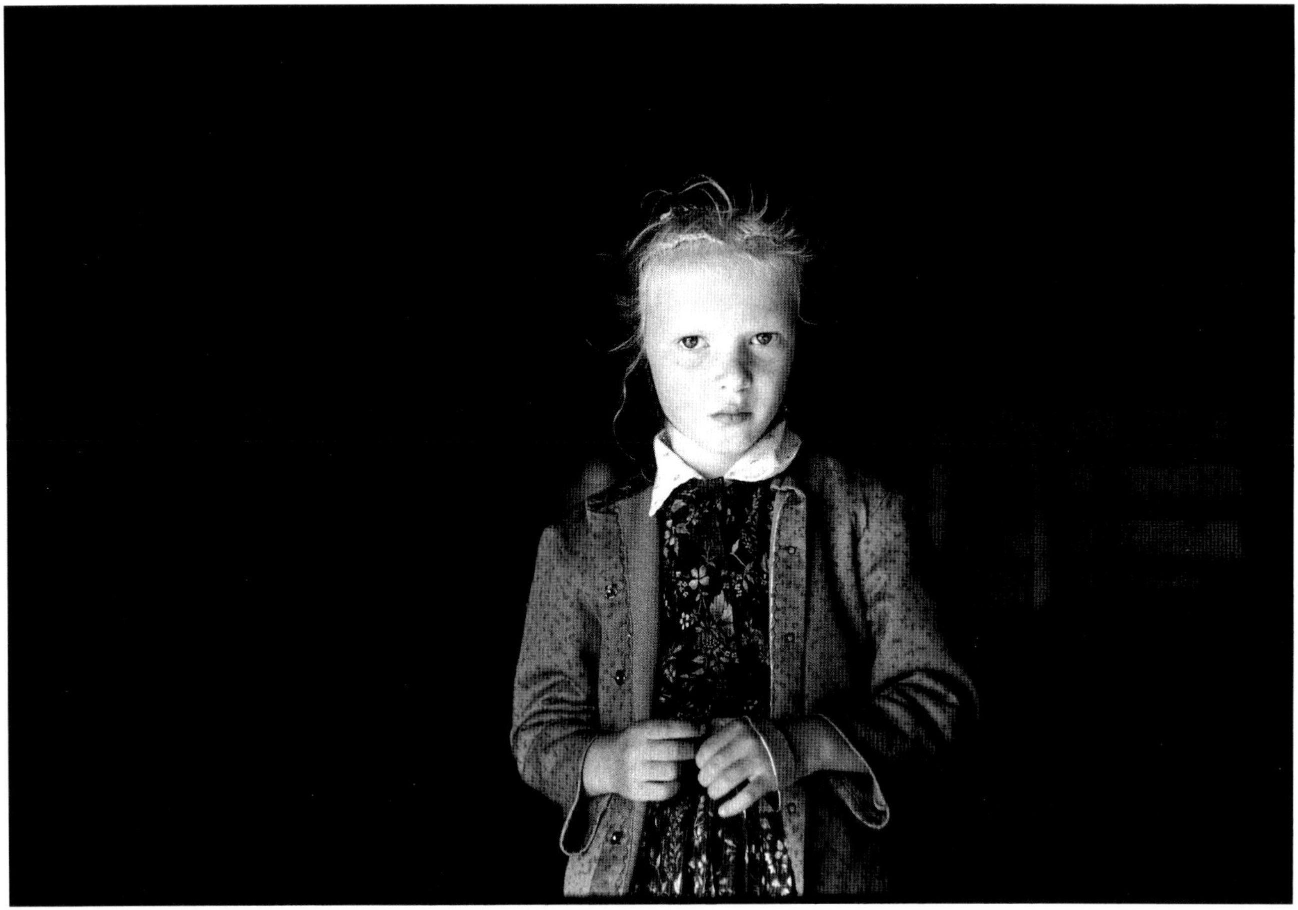

JUNE 5, 1999

I take a walk with two of Rebecca's grandchildren, Mathew, who is about thirteen, and his five-year-old sister, Sharon. As we walk she slips her tiny hand into mine. Mathew presents me with a gift from his grandmother, a pen inscribed with the name of her deceased husband, Mike.

AUGUST 1999

For the young girls it becomes a bit of a game ... who will hold "Uncle Garge's" hand on our walks around the colony. On one walk, little Sharon takes my right hand. Maria considers that to be her rightful place and bites Sharon on the forearm. Maria takes my right hand. Sharon cries for a bit, then takes my left hand as we continue our walk.

AUGUST 28, 1999

Joe Hofer, an elder member of the community and the former German teacher, is married to Kate. They sadly tell me of one of their sons who has left the colony and become a successful tradesman and contractor in the nearby city of Lethbridge.

SEPTEMBER 4, 1999

I am invited to say grace for the adults at the noon meal. After lunch there's a soccer game with the children. I score a goal.

Four of the teenage boys take me for a walk. We see the teepee rings, deer, and the confluence of the Little Bow River and Mosquito Creek.

SEPTEMBER 21, 1999

Five-year-old Sharon has a sliver in her foot. She's too upset to sit still when her mother, Ruth, attempts to extract it. She asks me to help by holding Sharon and cradling her head in my hands so that she will not look at the sliver being removed. Later that day, Sharon runs up to me with a slight limp and gives my leg a hug.

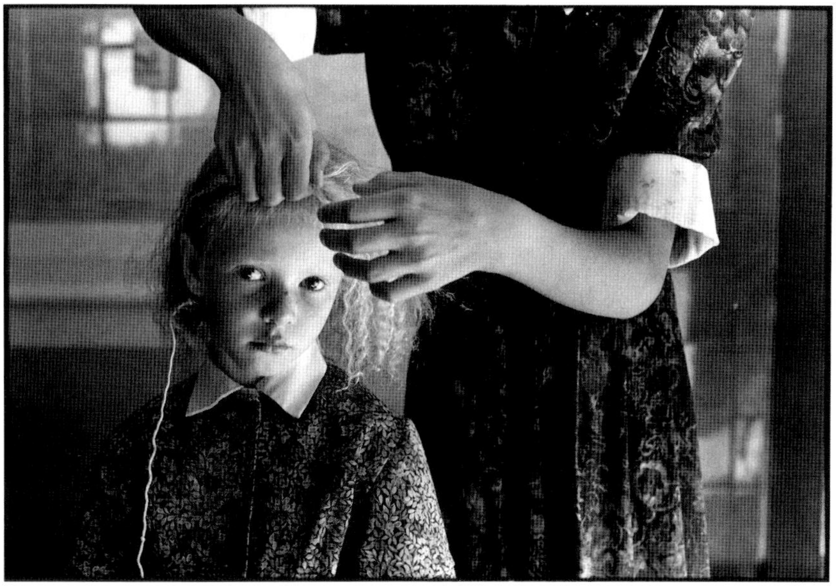

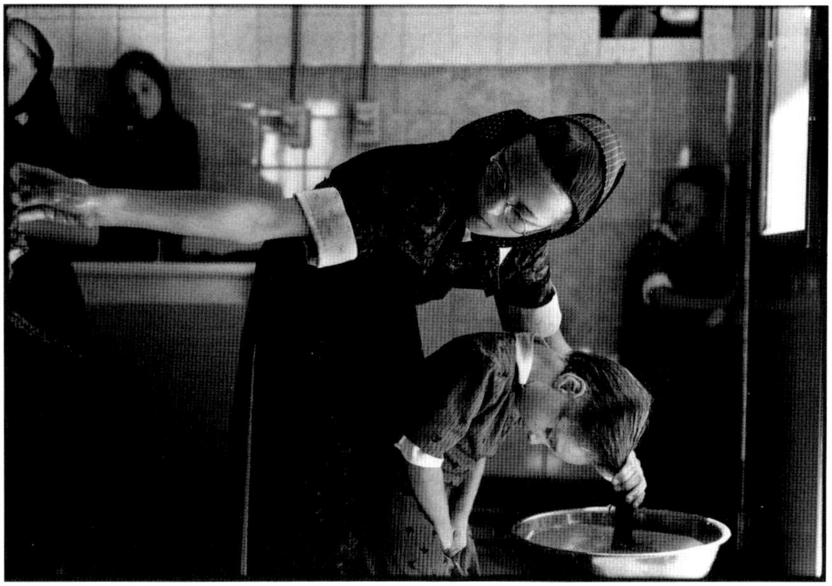

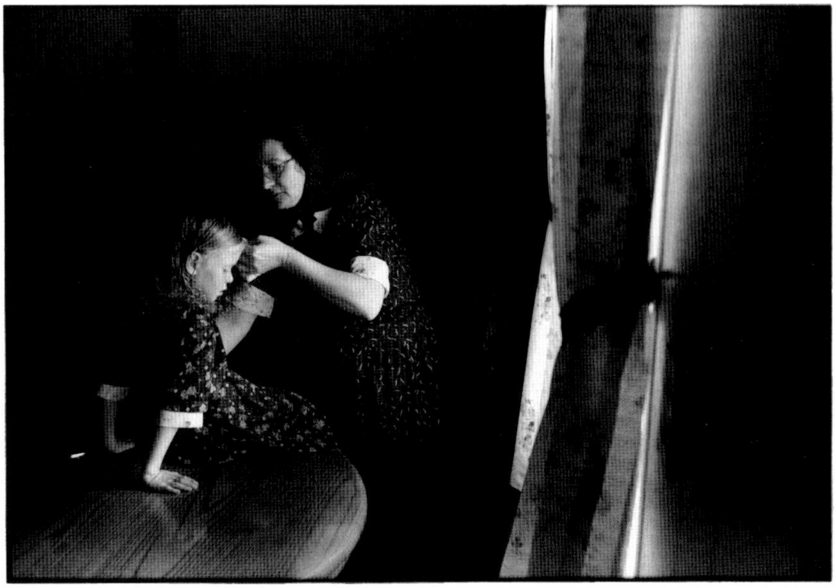

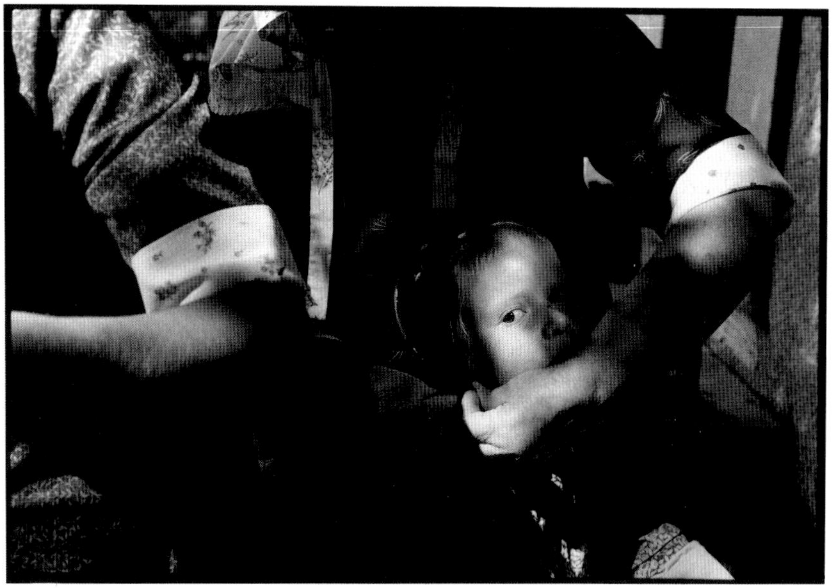

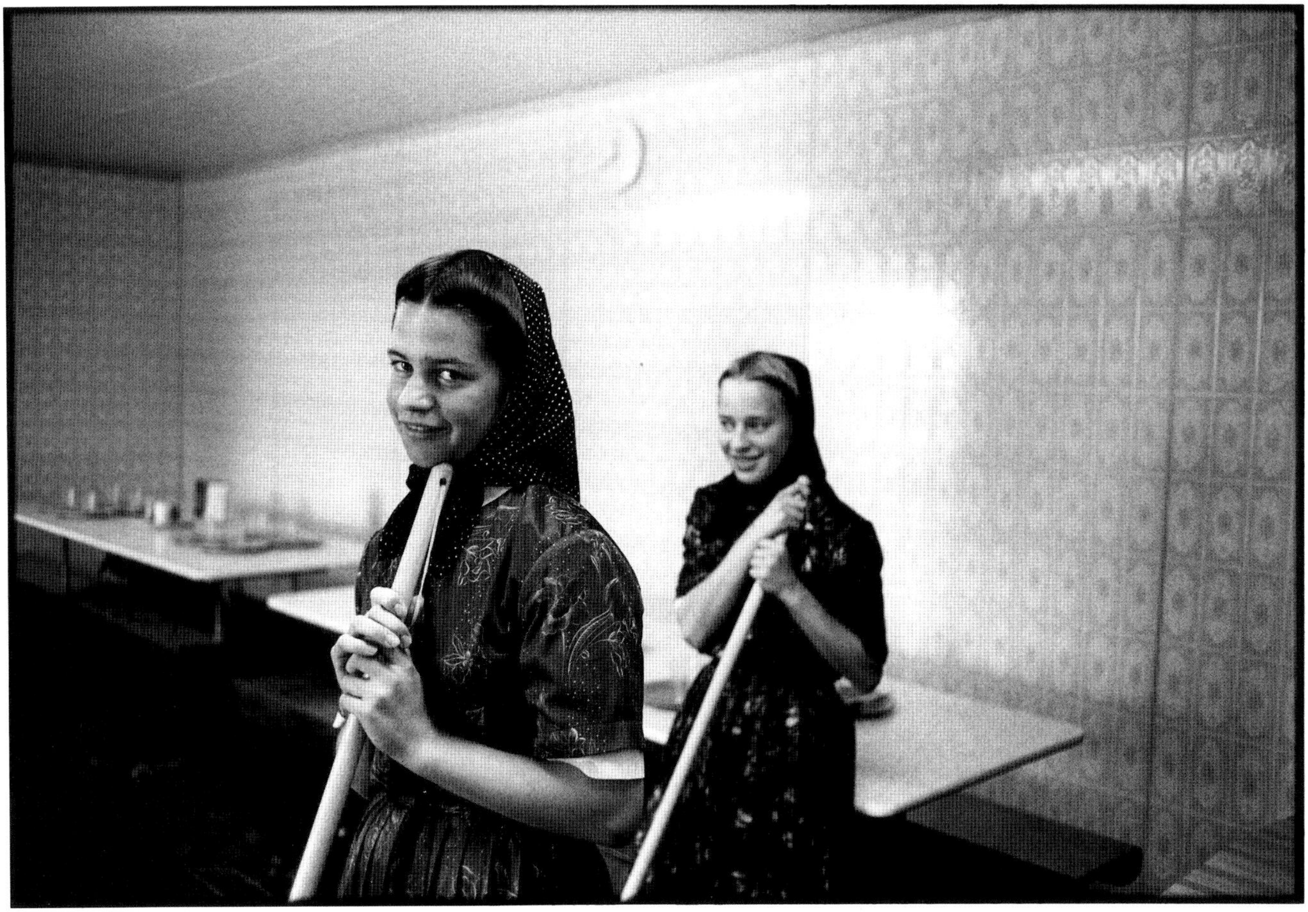

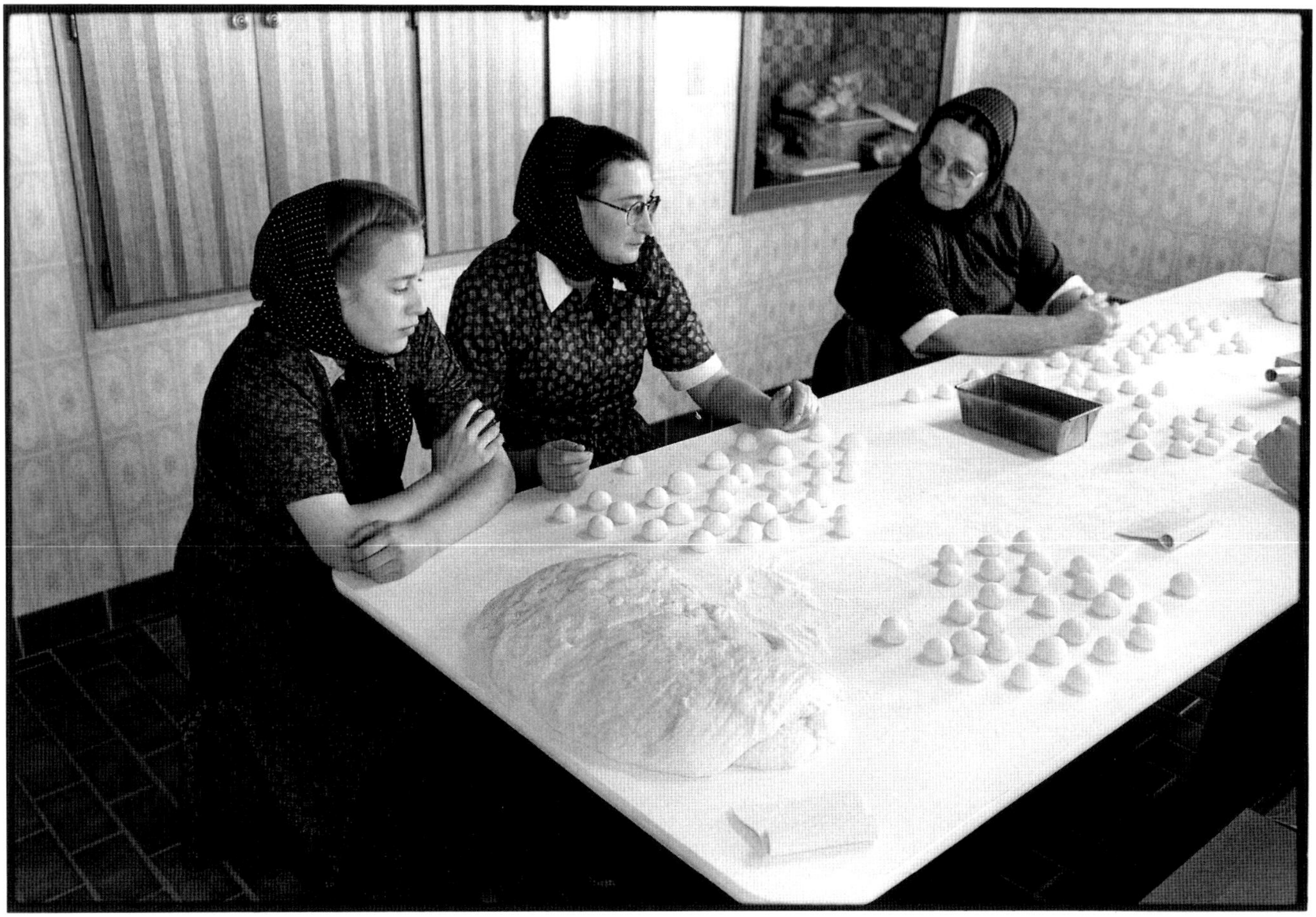

APRIL 21, 2000 (HOLY THURSDAY)

Walk with the children to see the new lambs. Katie asks me to say grace before the children's meal. Afterward they applaud. A drive out to see the new colony site with several of the boys. When we return Maria and Julie jump up on the running boards and hand me oranges through the open window.

SEPTEMBER 4, 2000

Double rainbow as I approach the colony. Grandpa Joe tells me that one of his brothers and one of his sisters have died since my last visit less than a month ago.

OCTOBER 13, 2000

After the midday meal I drive over to the new colony with several of the older boys and girls. They insist on the country music station—cranked all the way up. When we return Mathew gives me five of his drawings of animals. Then we go to see Wendy's five new kittens. Her father, Andy, has recently acquired "Blackie," a horse who is expecting a foal in the spring. Later, four of the grade one girls take me for a walk along the road while singing "Deep Water." When we return there's coffee with Paul and Ruth, who sends me home with a saskatoon berry pie. Driving home there's a big orange harvest moon in the rear-view mirror.

MAY 9, 2001

Dust storm turns midday into twilight with powerful winds from the north. Much talk and sadness surrounding the killing of five-year-old Jessica Koopmans in nearby Lethbridge last week.

SEPTEMBER 3, 2001

Visit with Annie and her husband. They have two children, Garry and Debbie. She sadly remembers the loss of two other children as babies. Annie agrees to make me a down comforter, telling me that she will work on it with the help of her sisters and mother when she visits them in their colony, which is north of here.

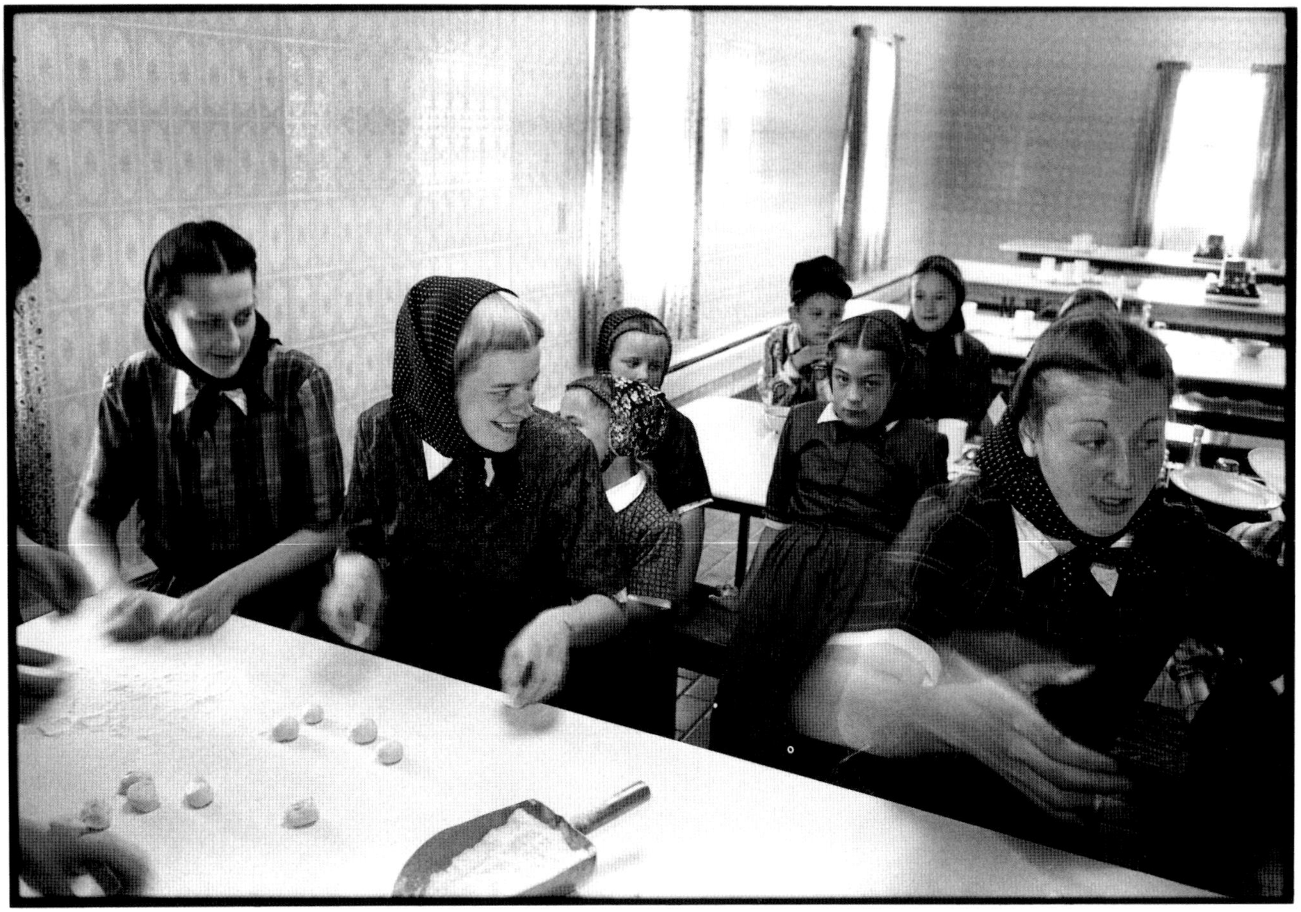

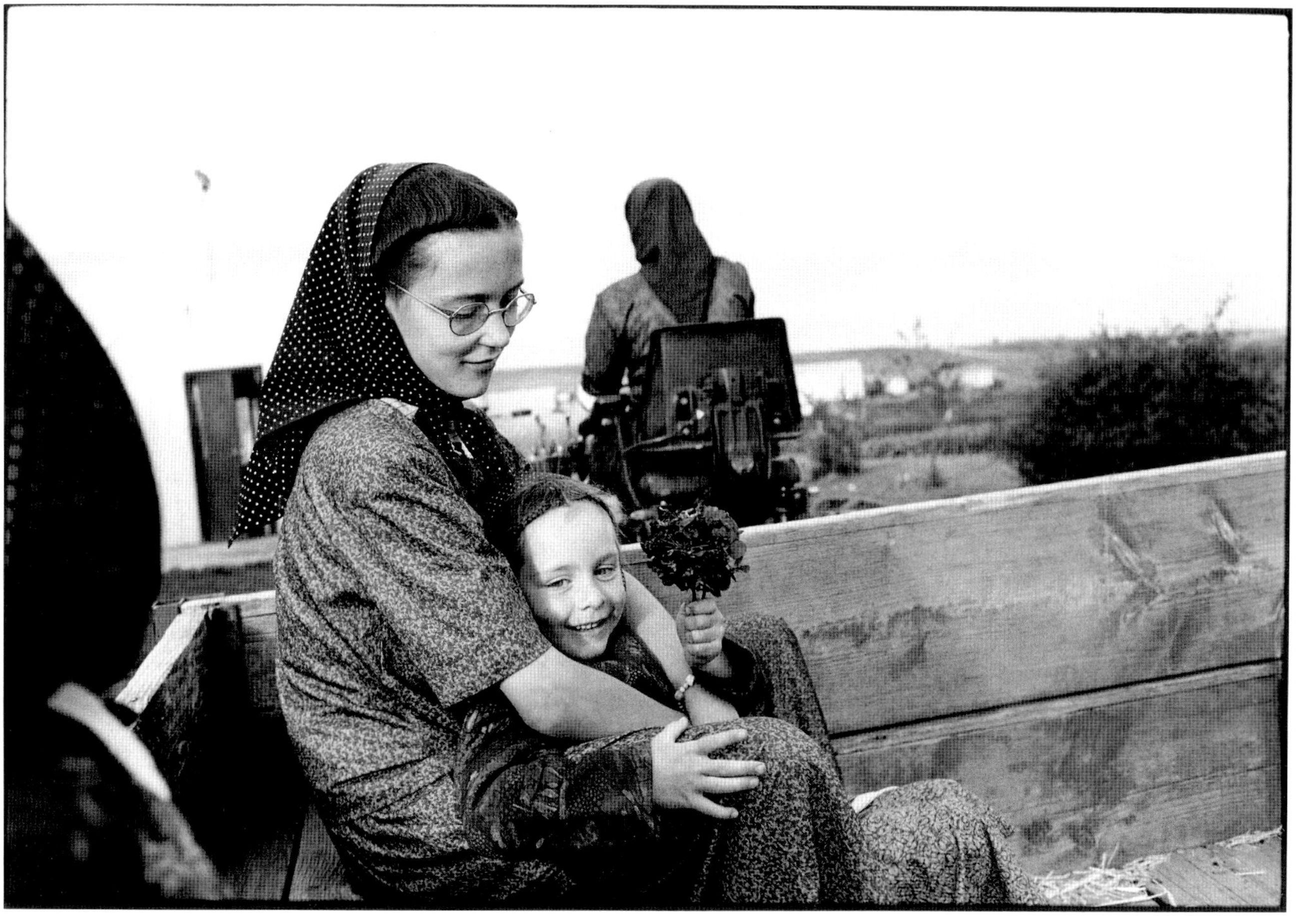

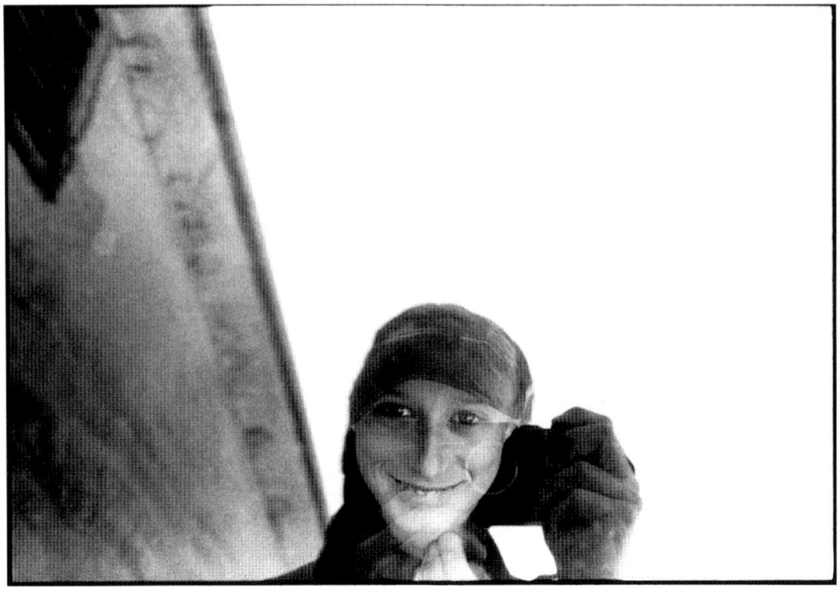

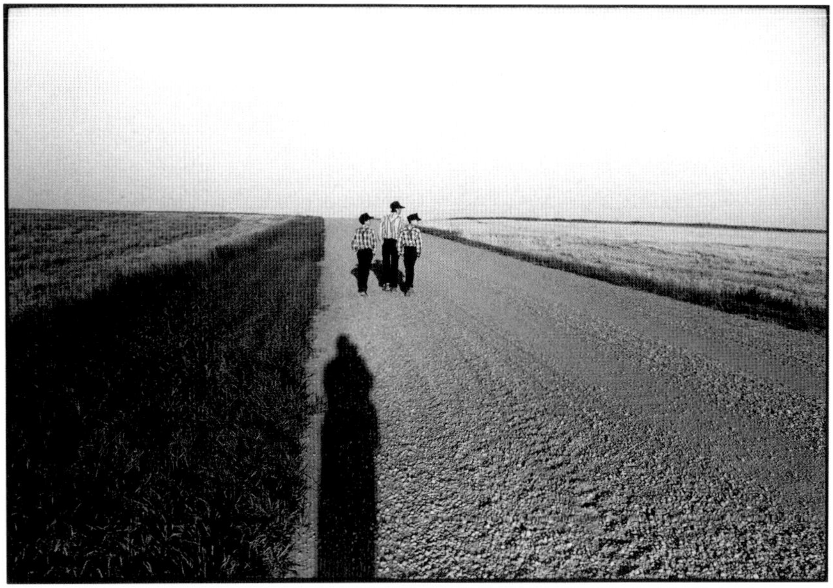

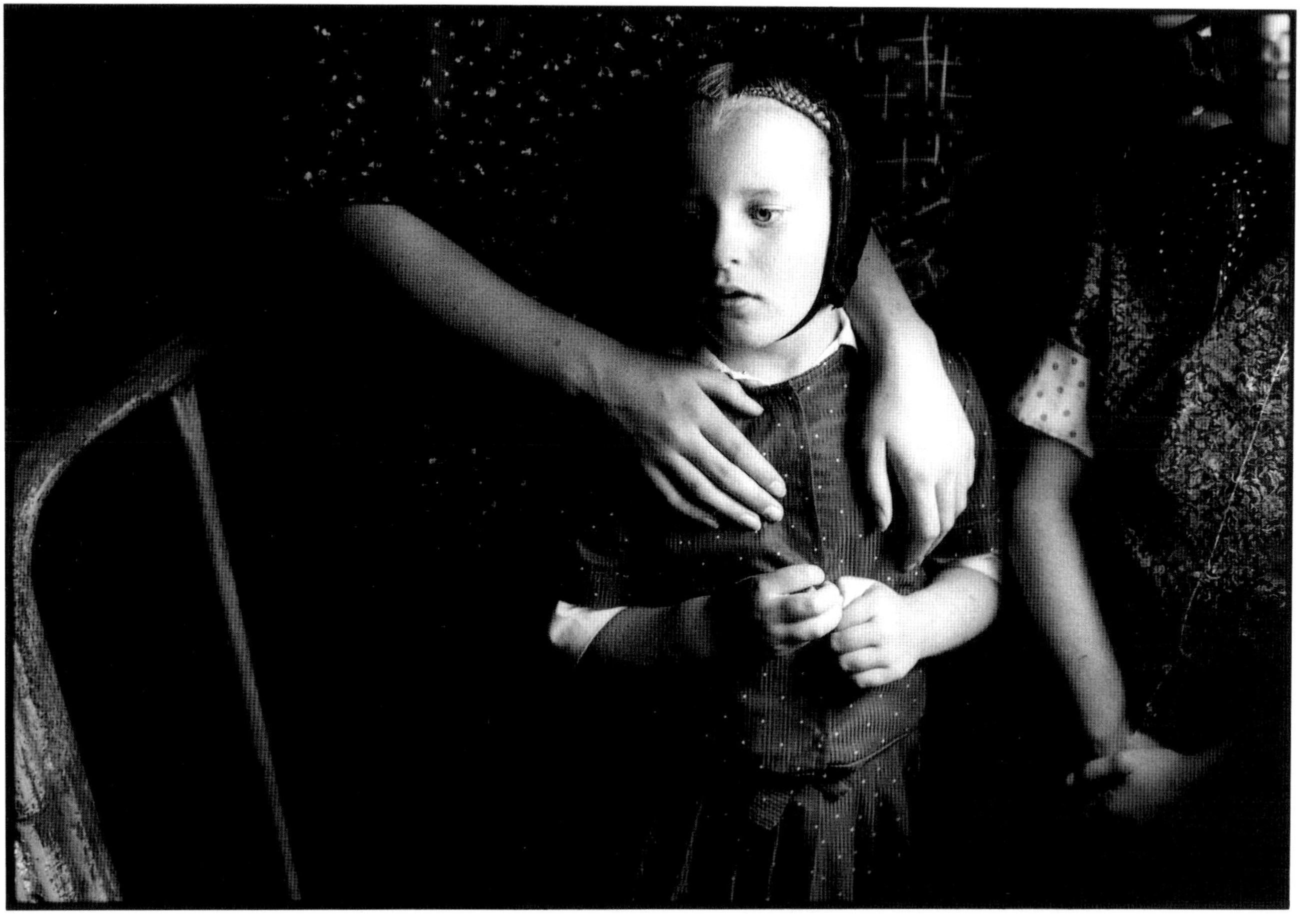

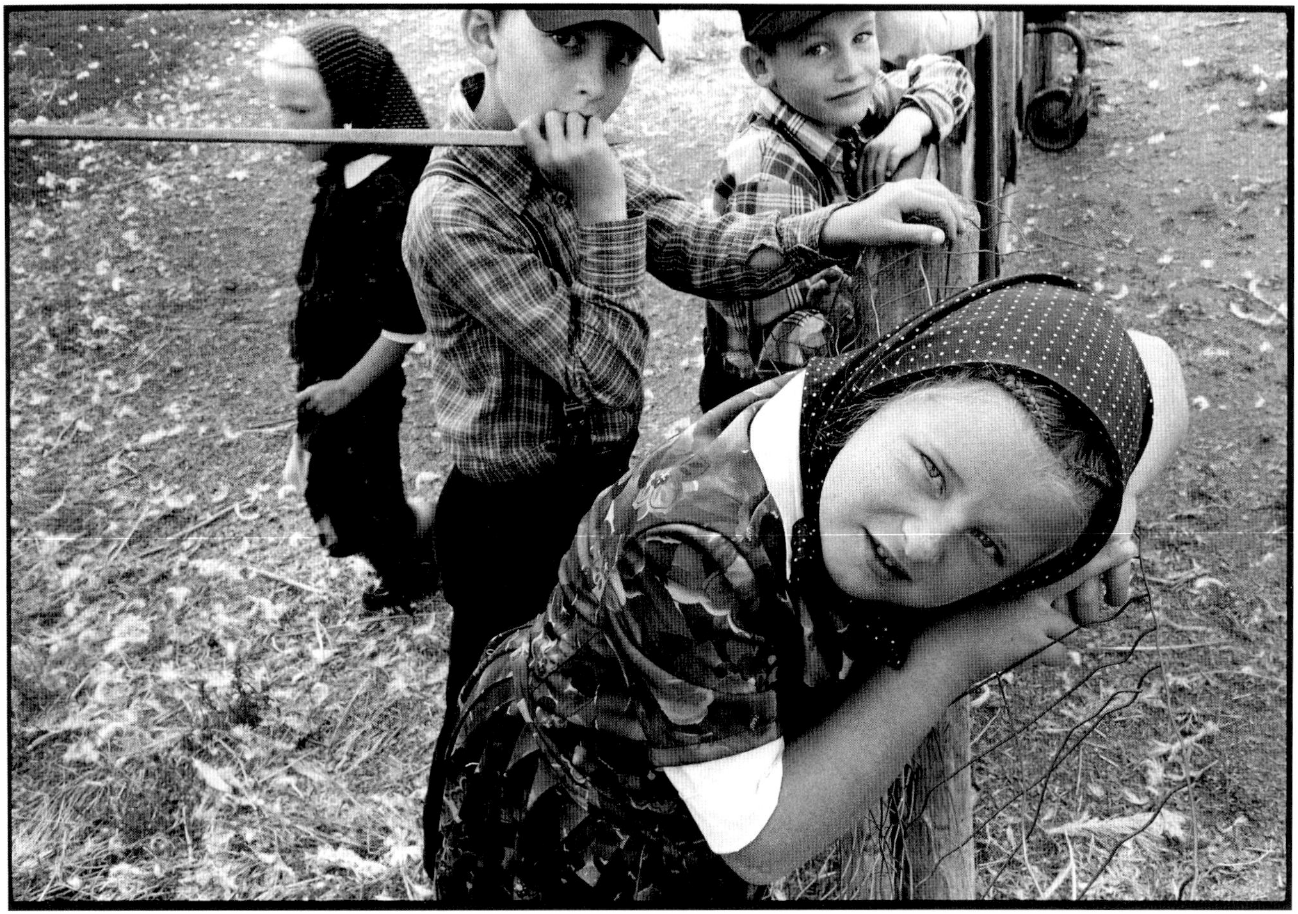

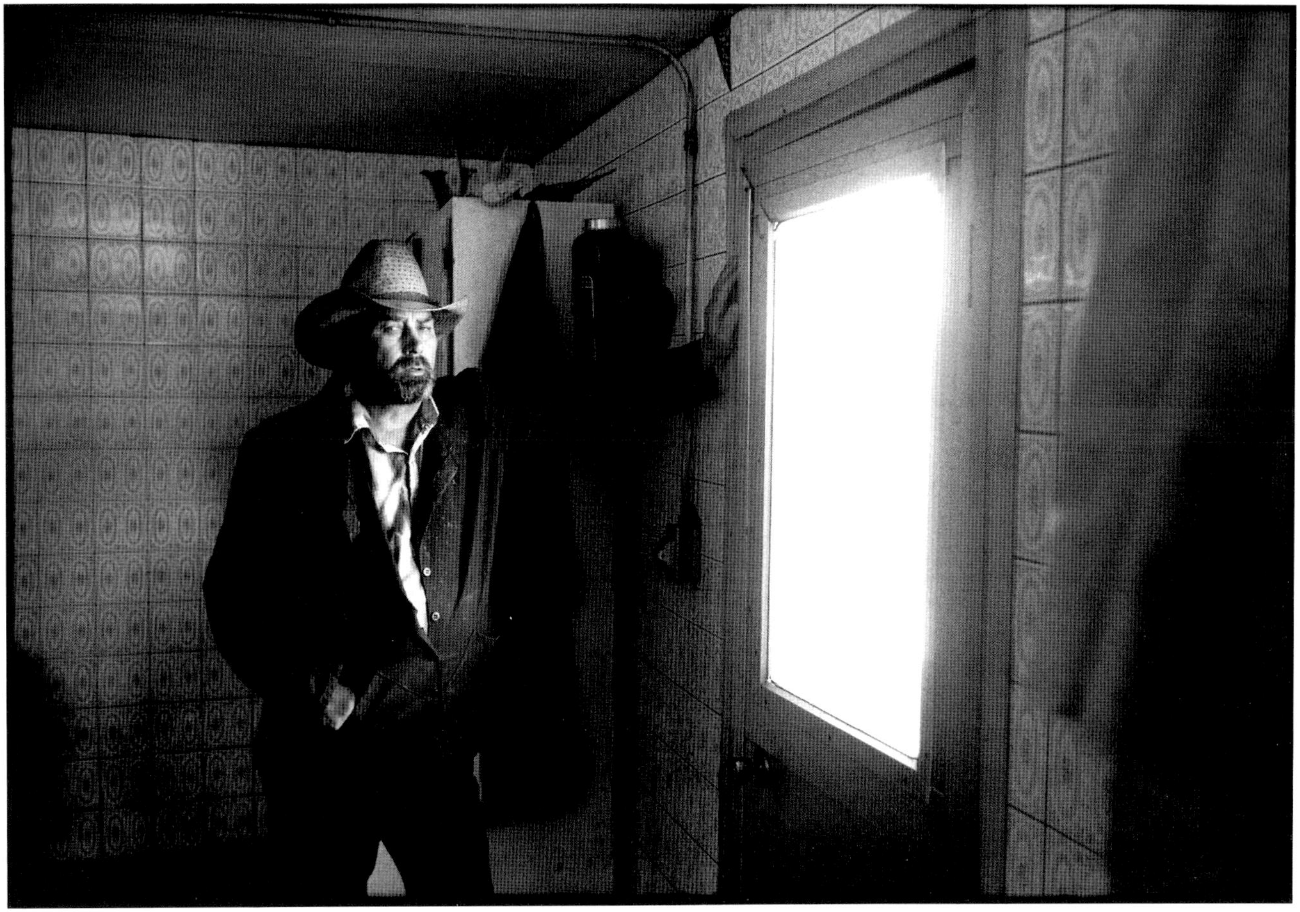

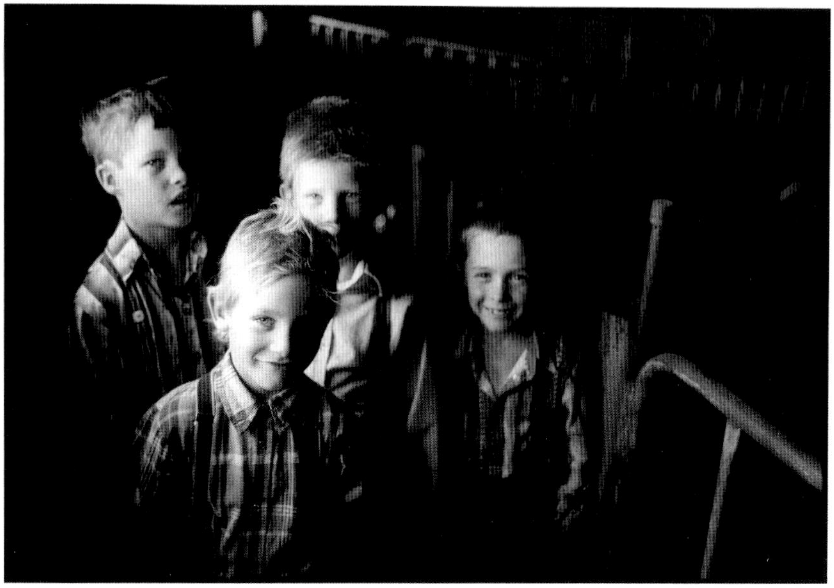

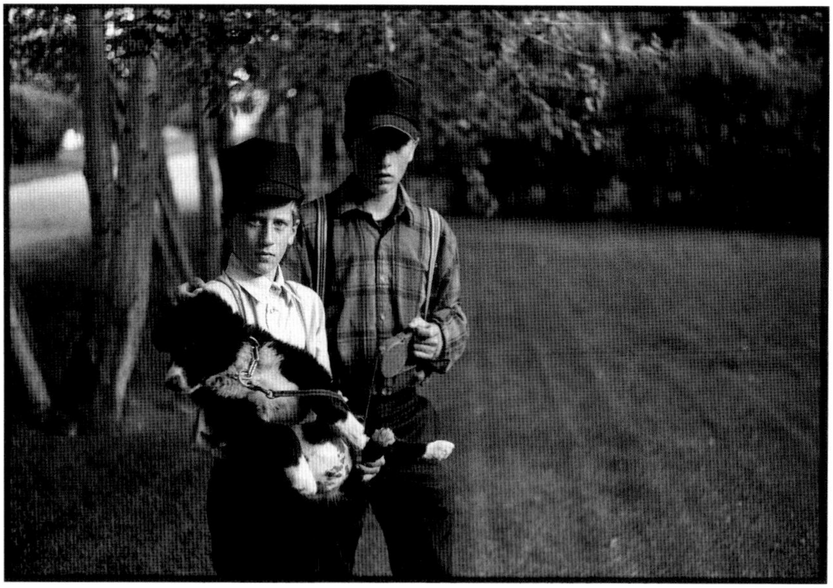

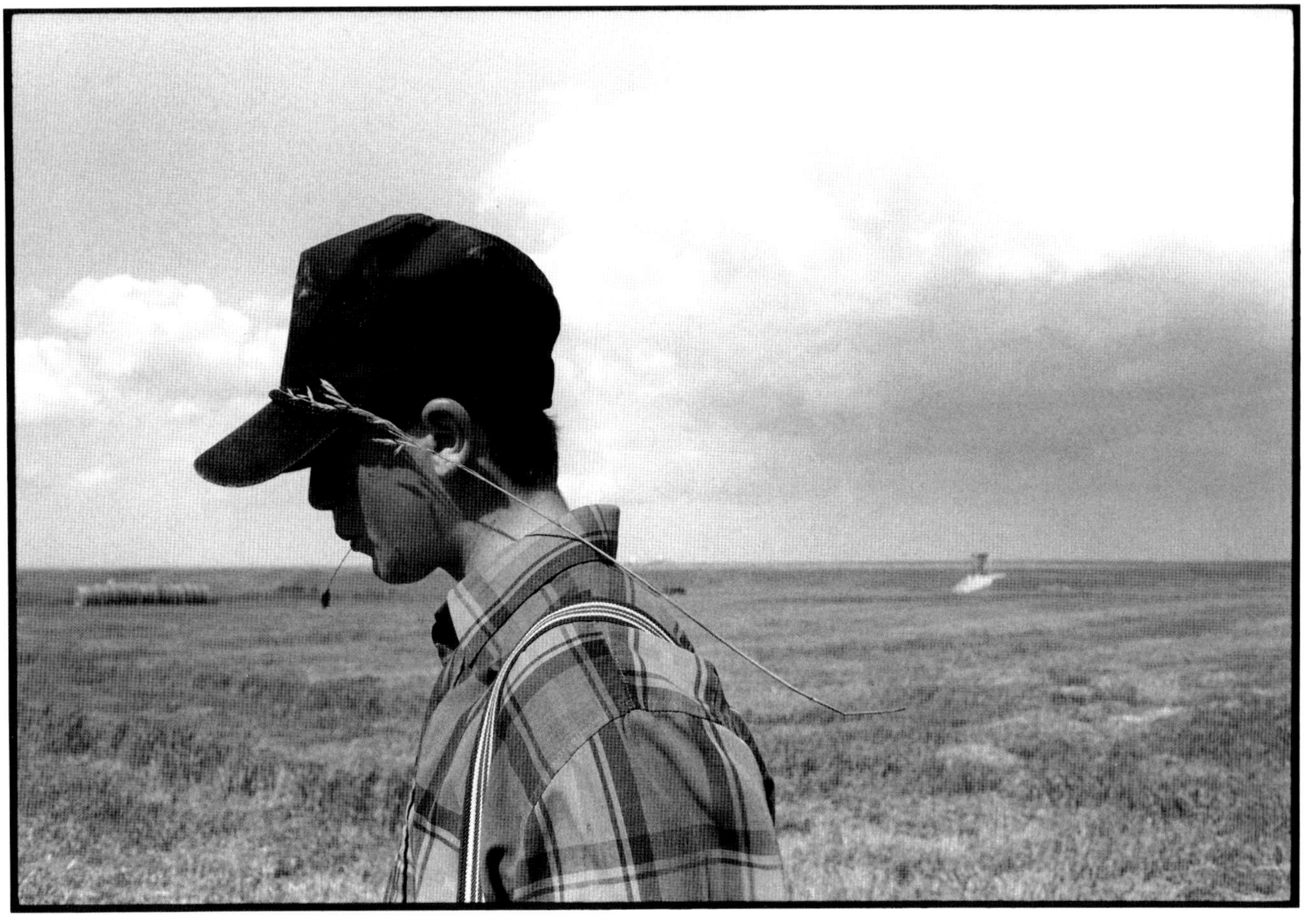

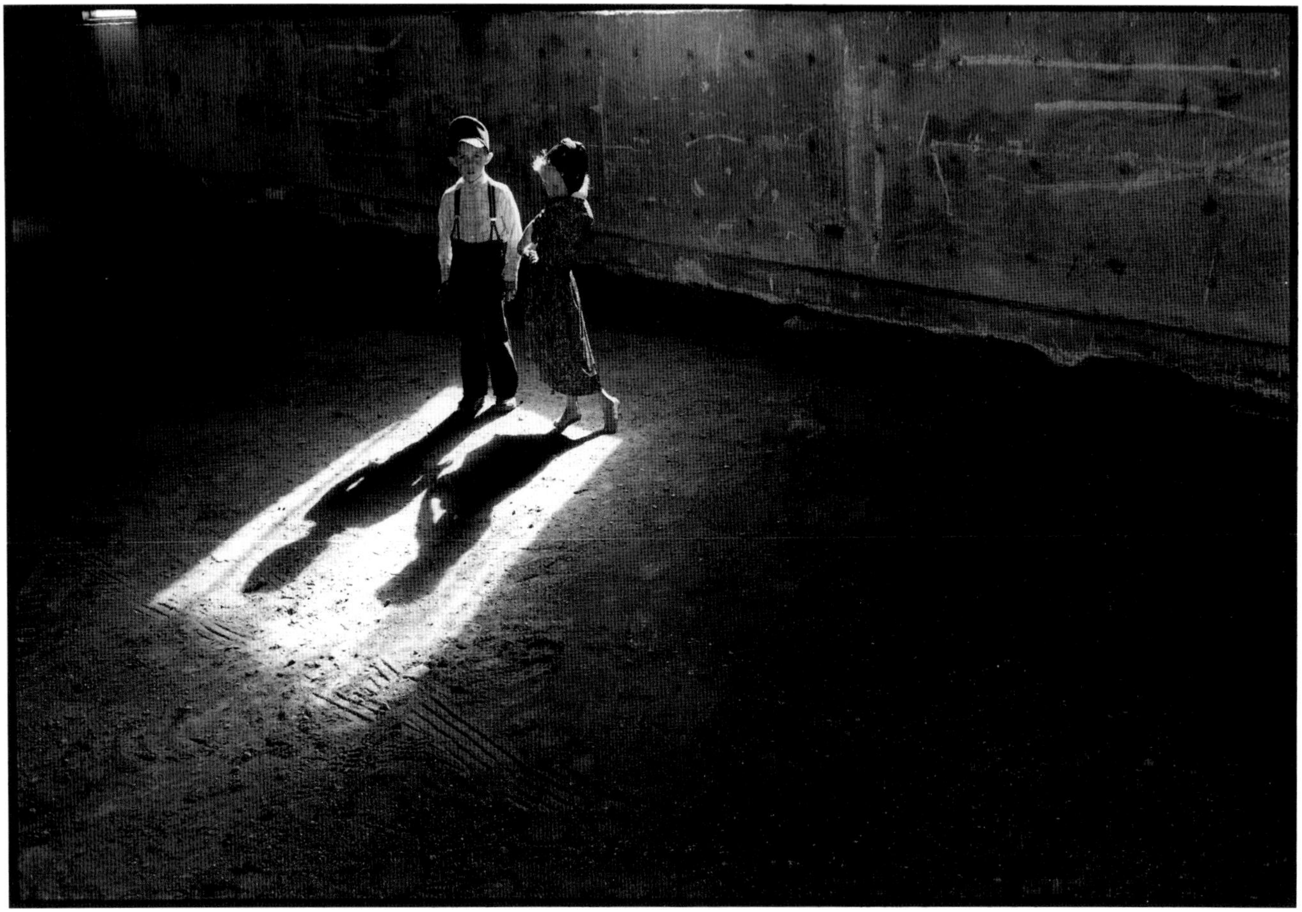

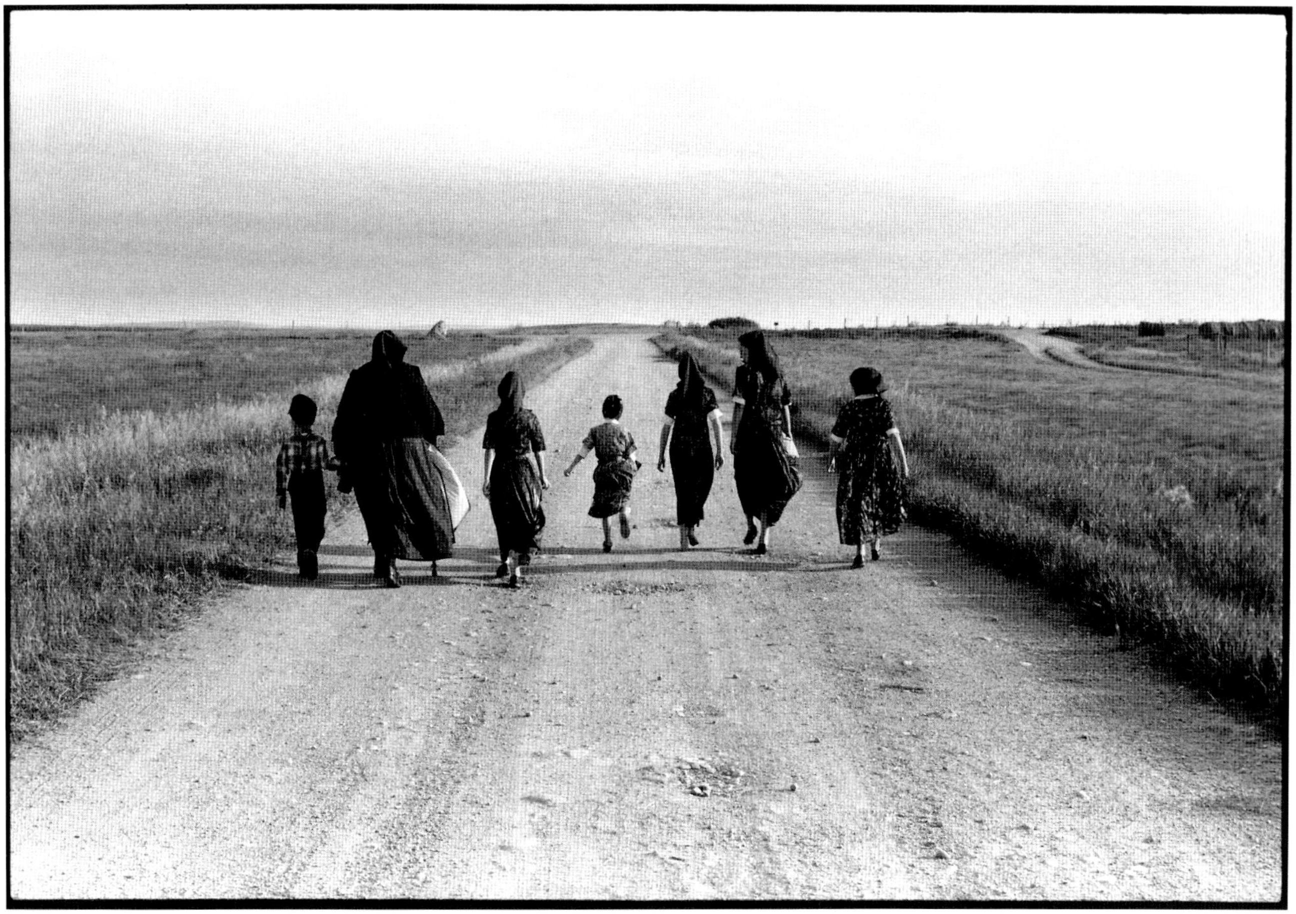

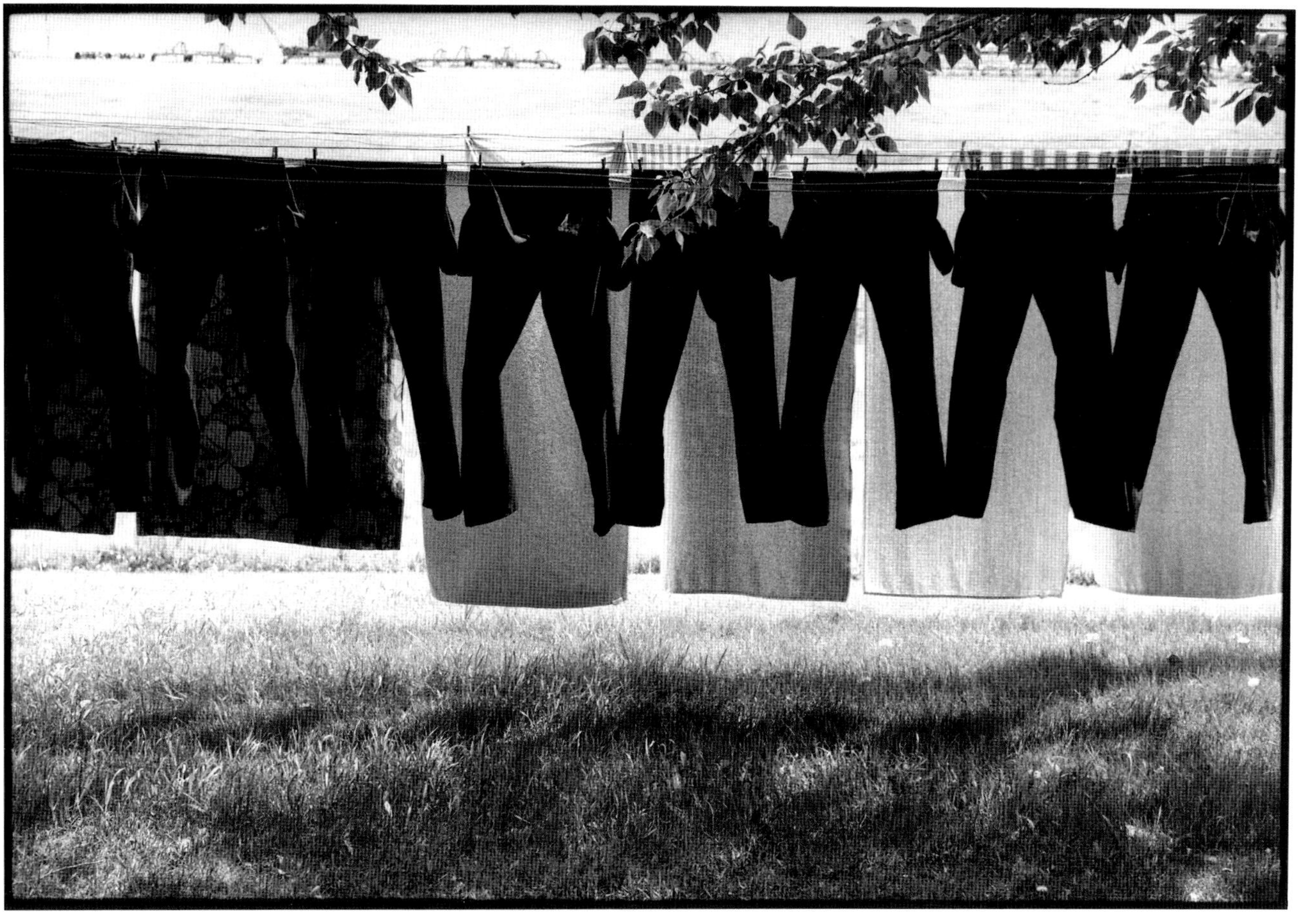

SHARING ALL THINGS IN COMMON

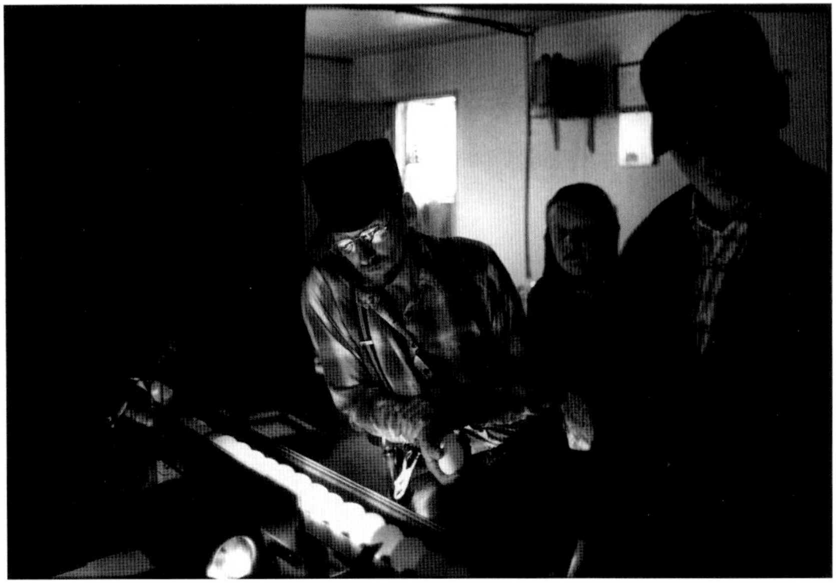

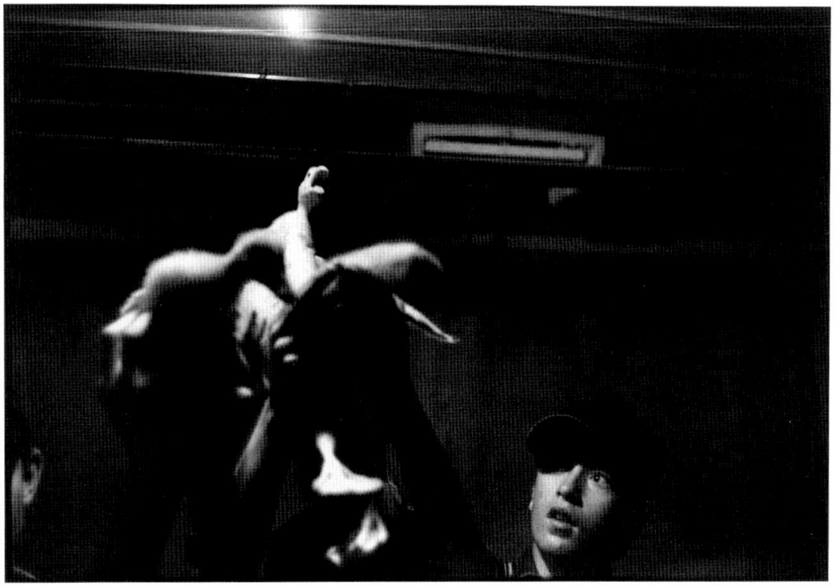

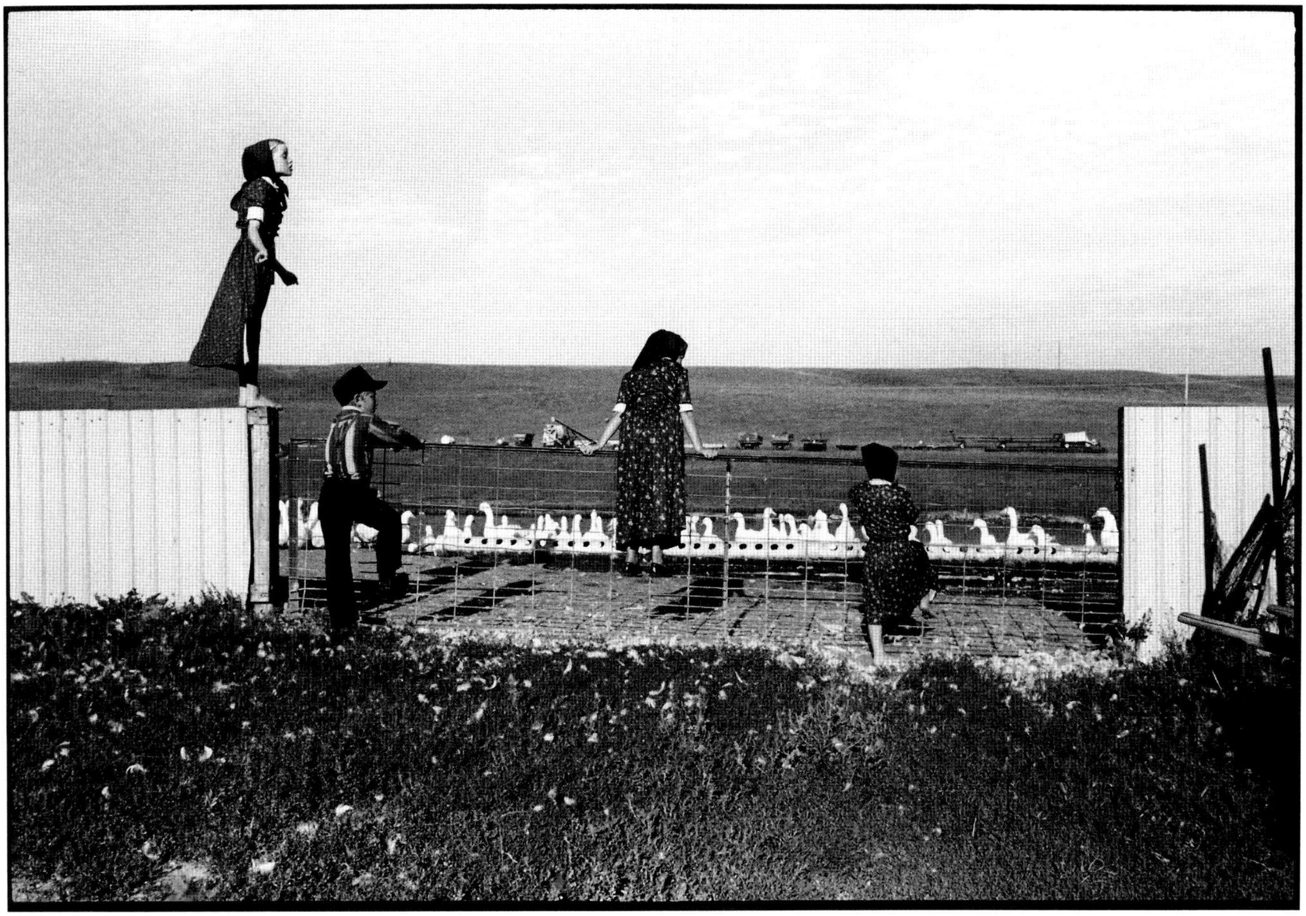

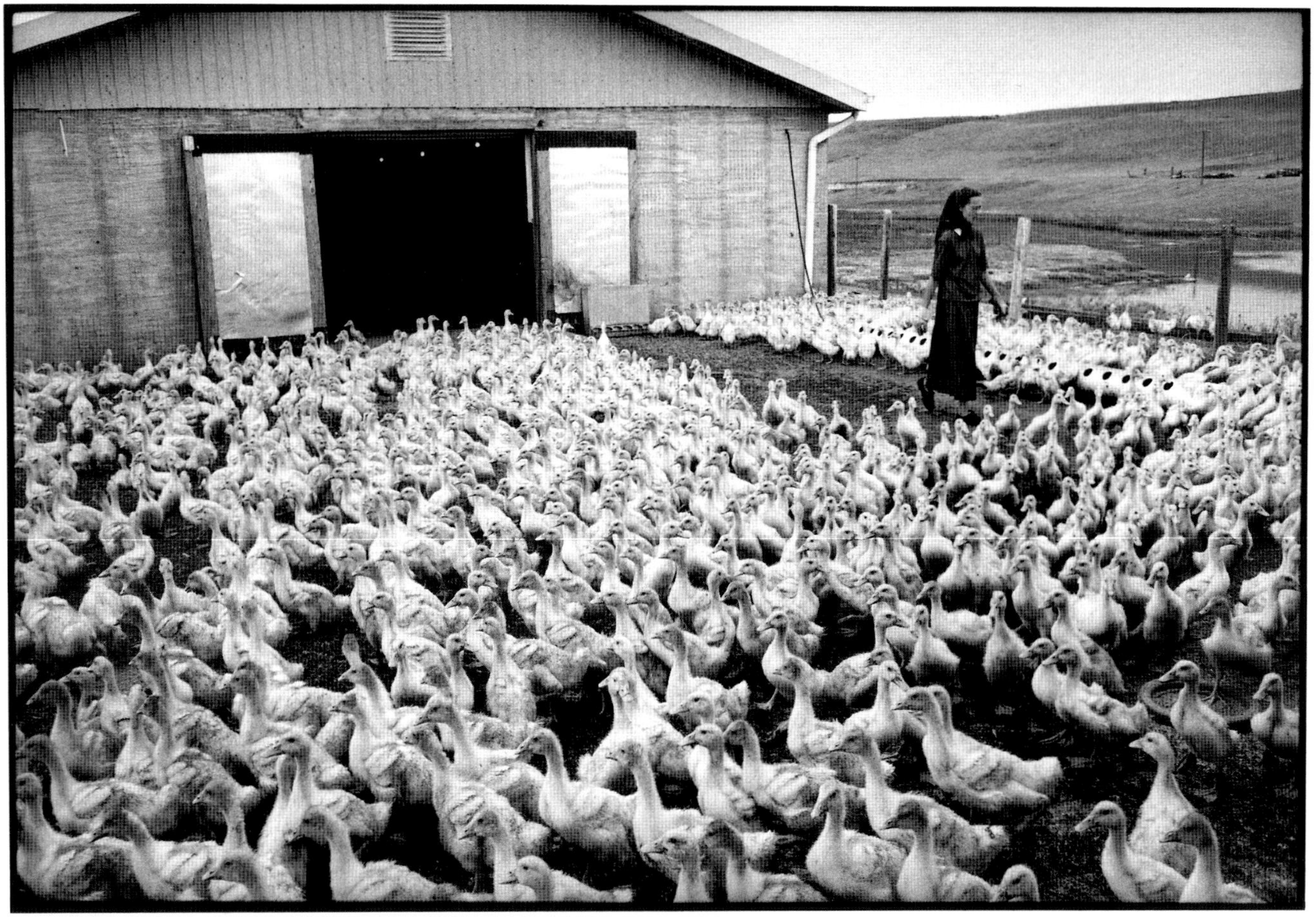

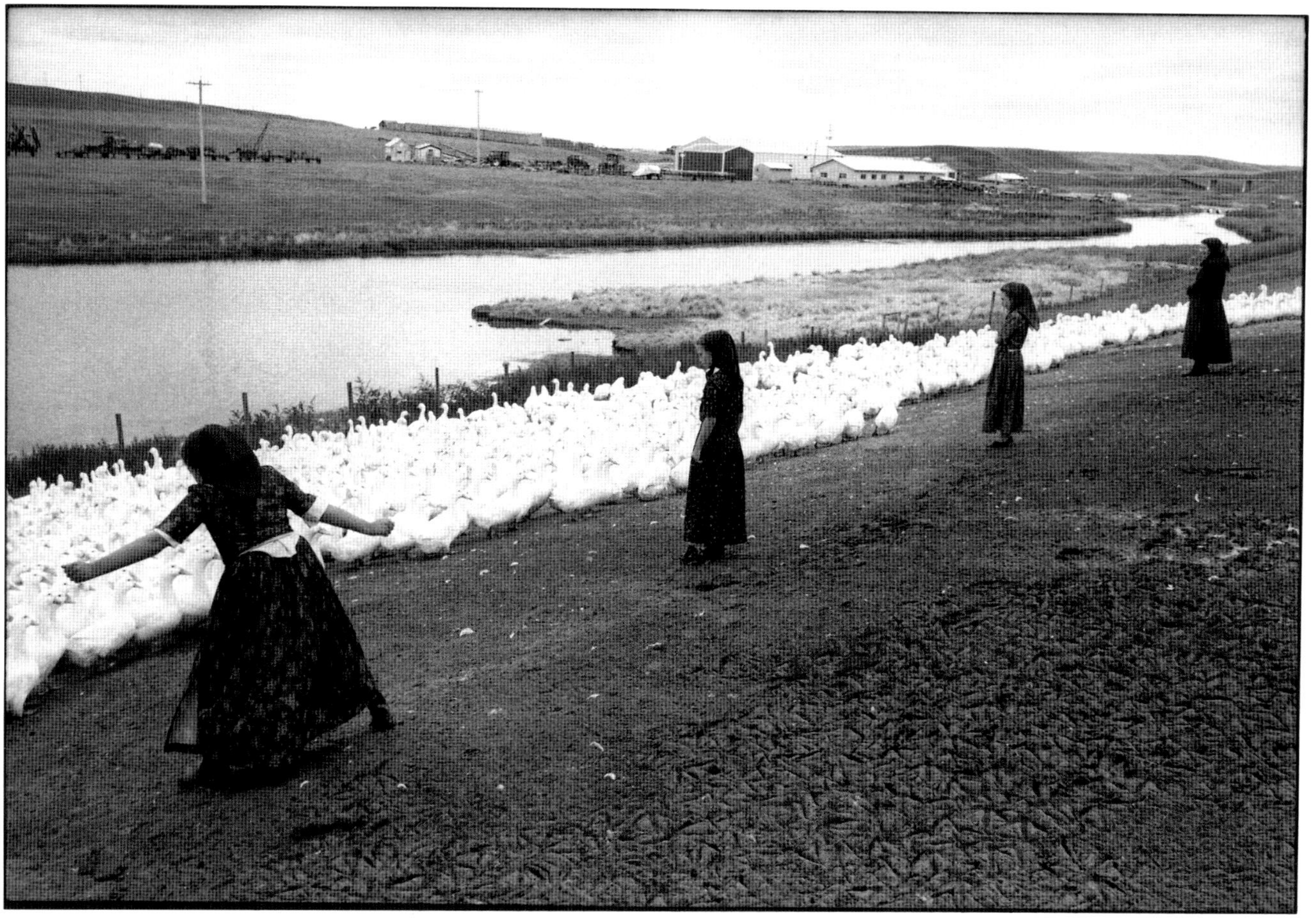

SEPTEMBER 21, 1999

Slaughter of the ducks—the brilliant scarlet pools of blood on the dark earth, the drudgery, the hard work, the humour, the efficiency ... the slaughter of five hundred white ducks ... slaughtering—beheading—steaming—plucking—waxing—plucking for a second time—washing—eviscerating—soaking—cooling—then freezing. All members of the colony aged fifteen and over work from 7:00 AM to 3:00 PM to prepare the five hundred ducks. There will be four hundred more to do in two days.

FEBRUARY 2, 2000

Sheep shearing in the automotive maintenance shop. Paul jokingly asks me if I want a haircut. Approximately 120 sheep are sheared in three hours.

Trip with the seven Hutterite women to see the new colony construction.

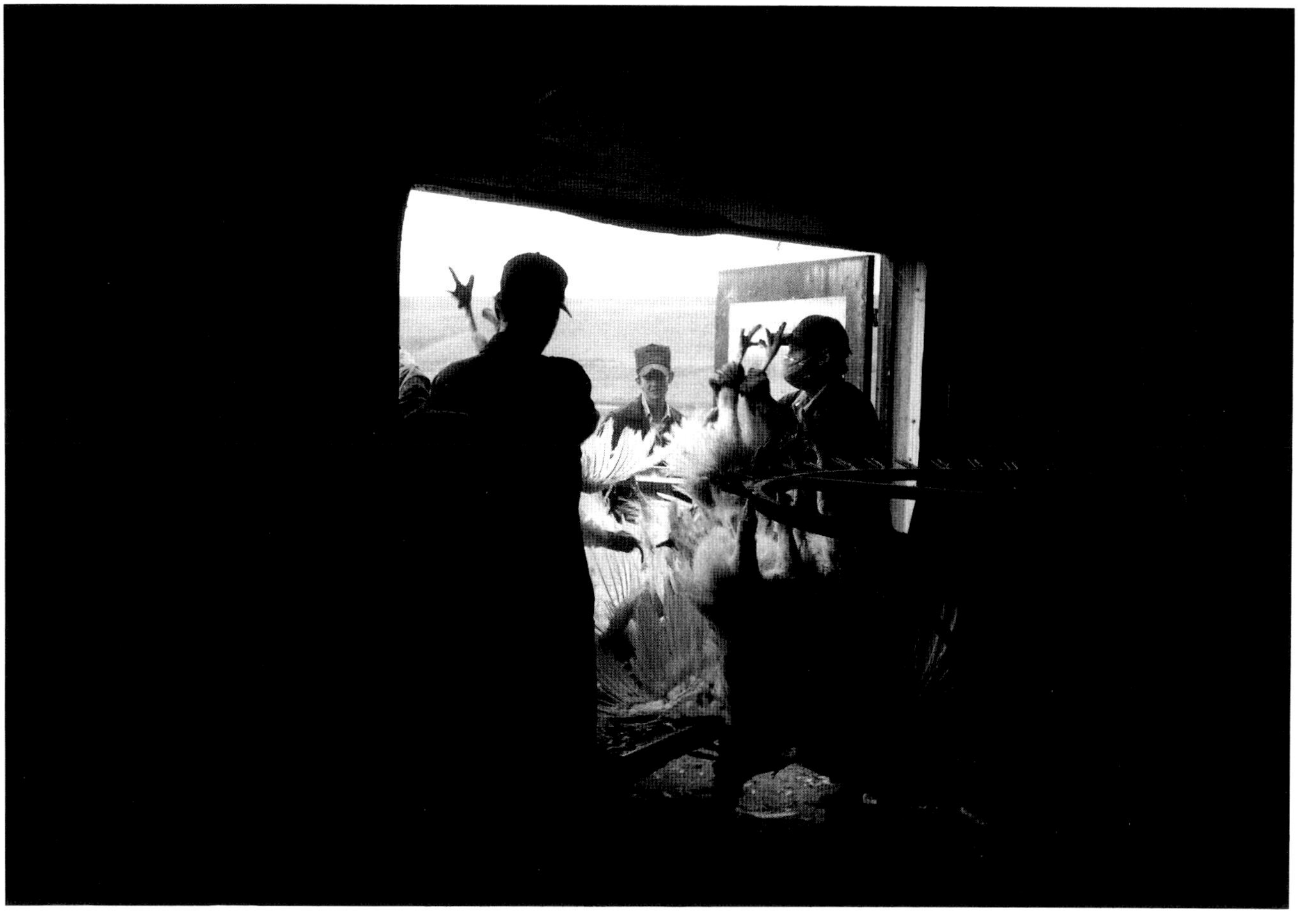

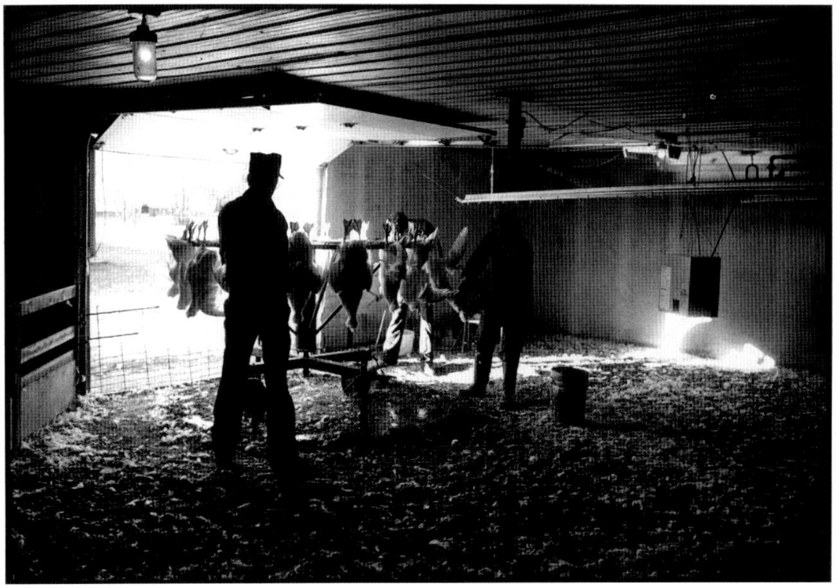

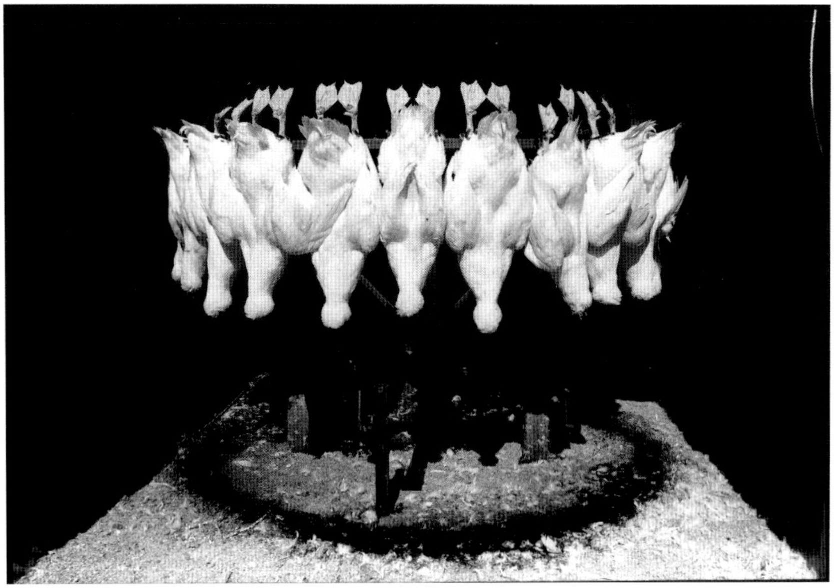

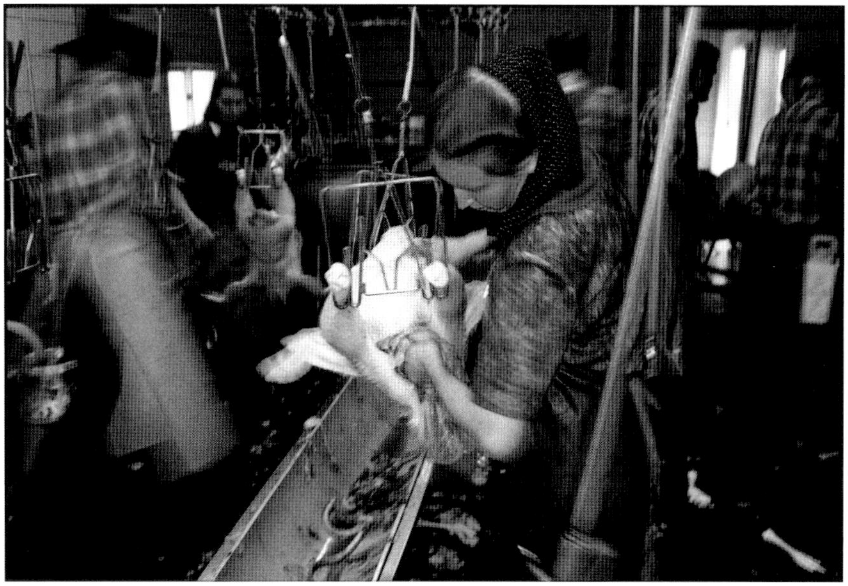

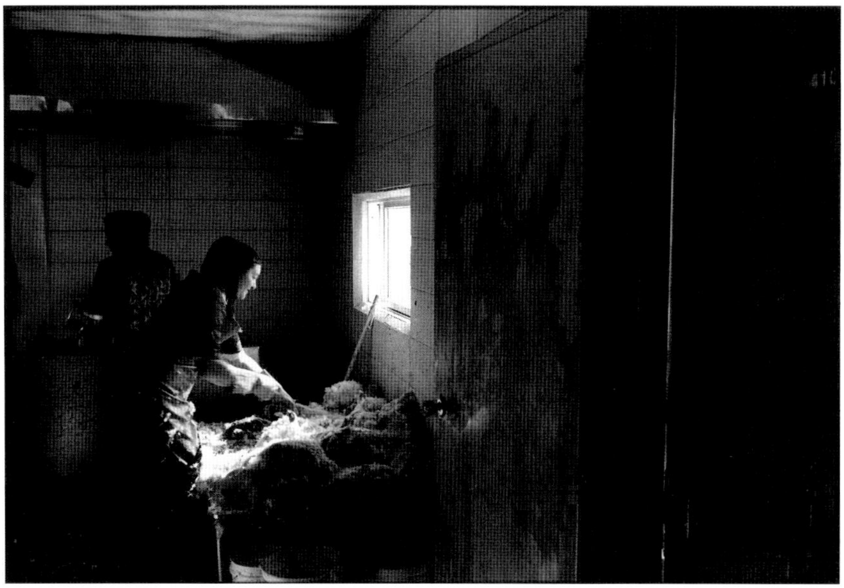

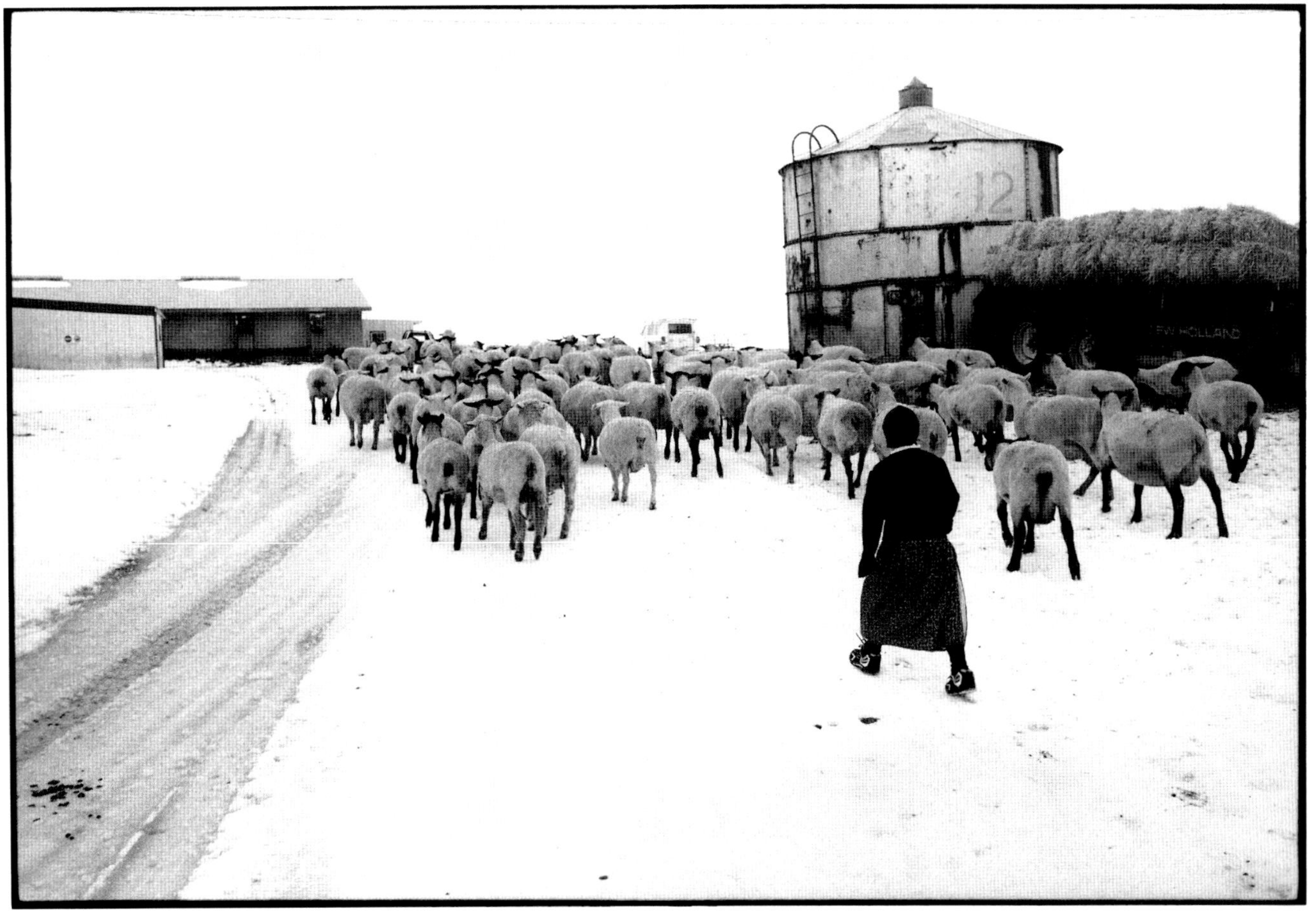

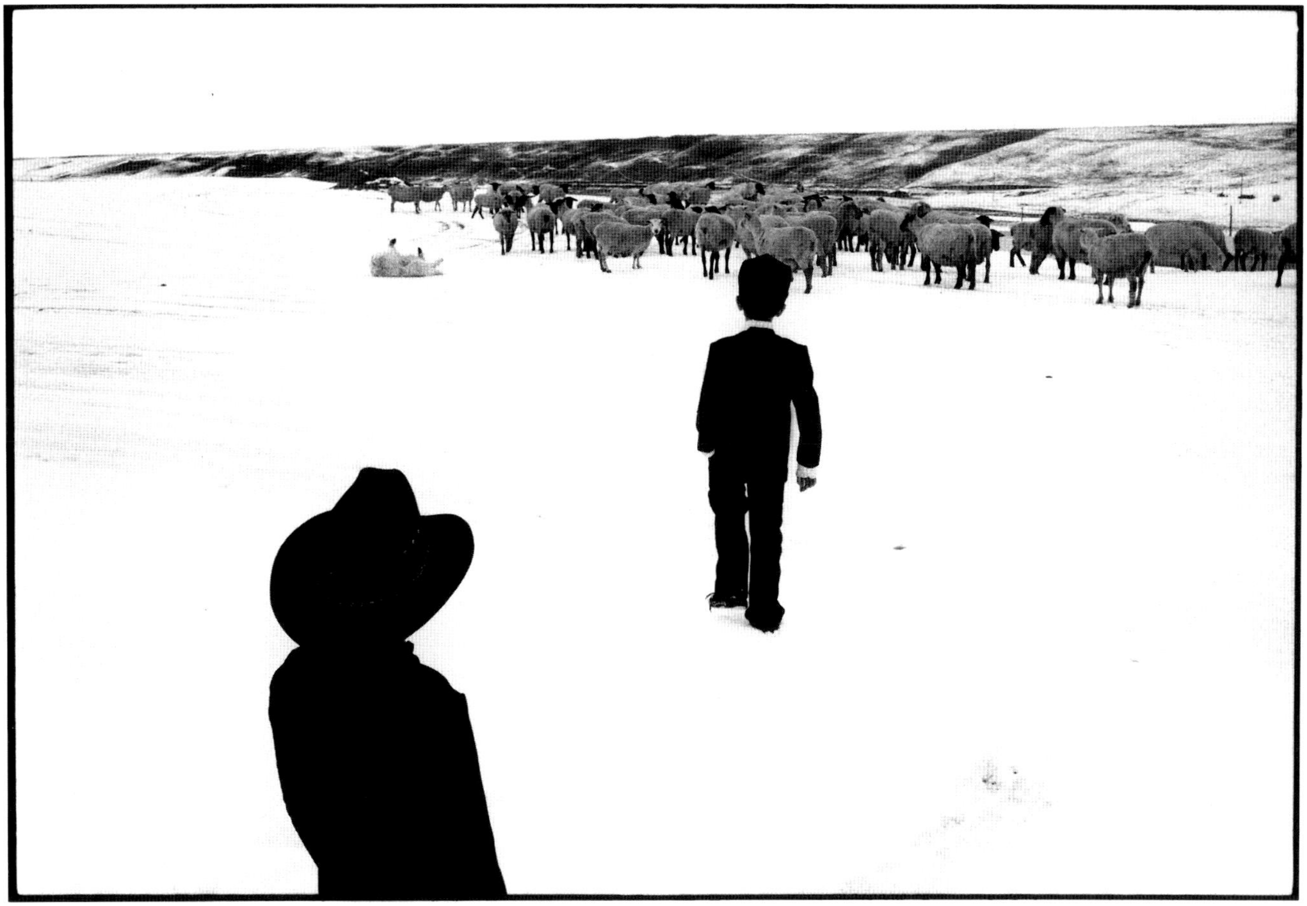

FEBRUARY 3, 2000

Hog slaughtering and butchering: I arrive before sunrise. Preparations are already underway for the slaughter of ten hogs. A large truck sits in the snow-dusted garden. Just as the sun breaks the horizon, a cable is fastened to the hog's back leg and it is hoisted off the ground by a small tractor. Mike Hofer makes a clean, sure stroke across the hog's throat with his gleaming knife. A trail of blood traces the hog's path to the butchering area. First it's dropped into a large tub of boiling water to soften the hide and then into a rotating drum that pulls the hide away. The carcass is then lifted onto a hook, the body cavity opened, and the viscera drawn out. The sun hits billowing clouds of steam silhouetting the dark figures as they work swiftly and efficiently. One hog head after another is lined up on a heavy plank table. Some parts of the hogs are cut into pieces; others are boiled and run through a grinder to produce bright red tubes of liverwurst for the meal table.

FEBRUARY 21, 2000

Paul and Mike Hofer cut a large rectangular hole out of the frozen Little Bow River with a chainsaw in order to pump water into the colony's holding pond. Several of us push the truck that had gotten stuck taking the pump down to the river. Near sunset I start for home.

JUNE 11, 2000

Help the poultry man "Jonti" Hofer and the children prepare the duck barn with straw for the arrival of the ducklings.

JUNE 12, 2000

After meal with children, Katie tells me that I should get married so that my wife could prepare me a duck dinner. Helped Katie and the children harvest radishes. We all receive a stick of gum for helping out. I later hear that Paul's son Steve has left the colony and is now working harvesting wheat in Texas.

OCTOBER 13, 2000

Driving down into the valley I see Pete and a group of perhaps a dozen women taking in the last of the carrot crop. They glance up at sound of my approaching vehicle and in unison extend a welcoming wave. I park the truck. Katie shakes my hand and then in front of everyone gives me a big hug.

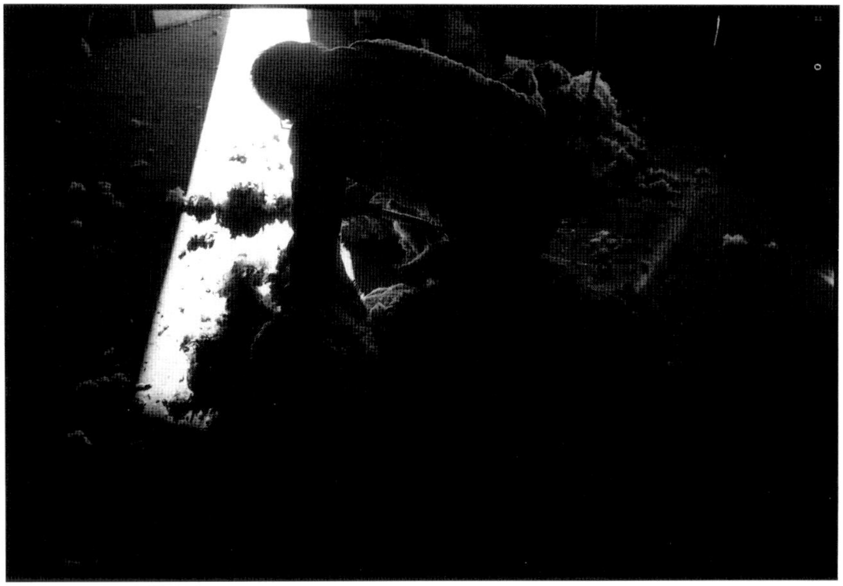

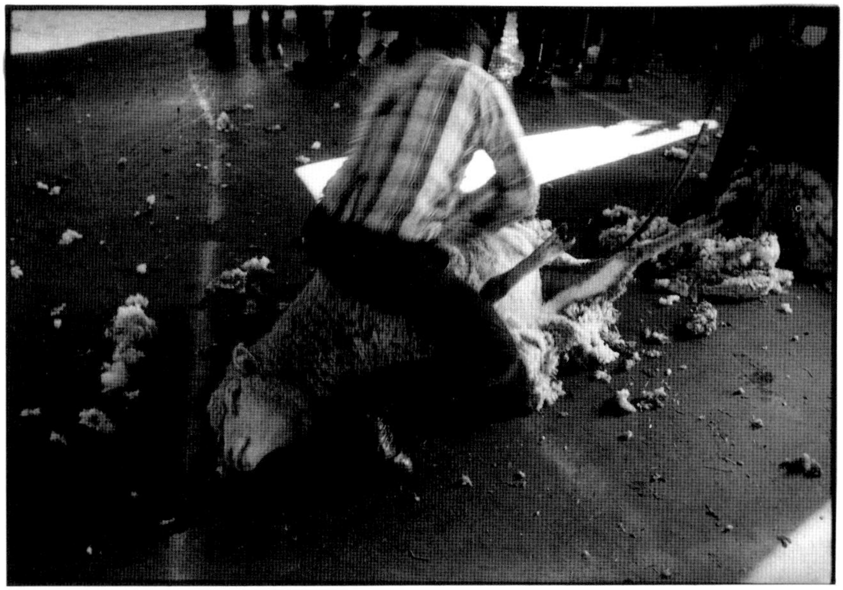

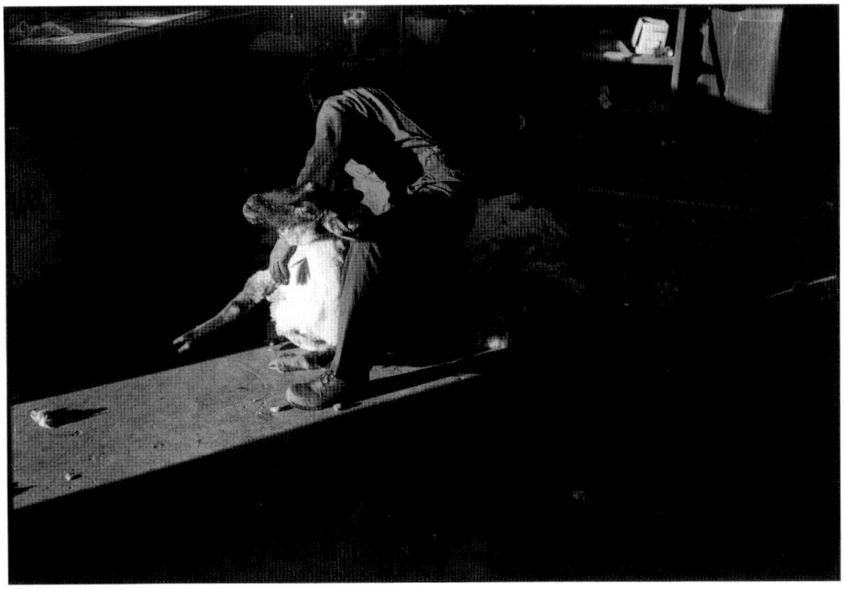

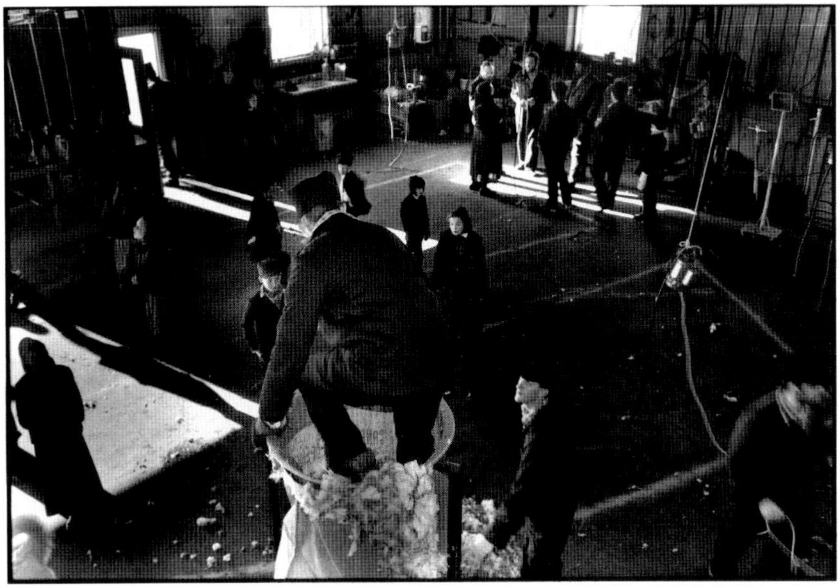

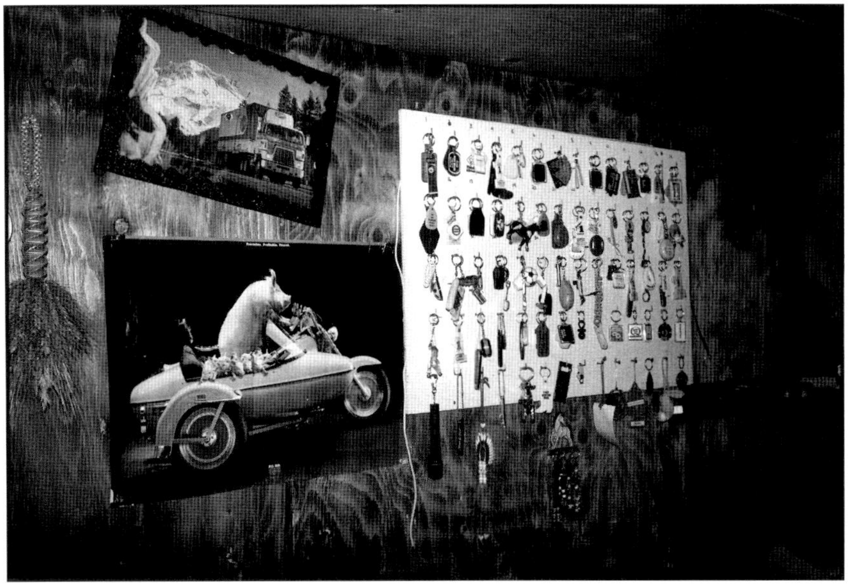

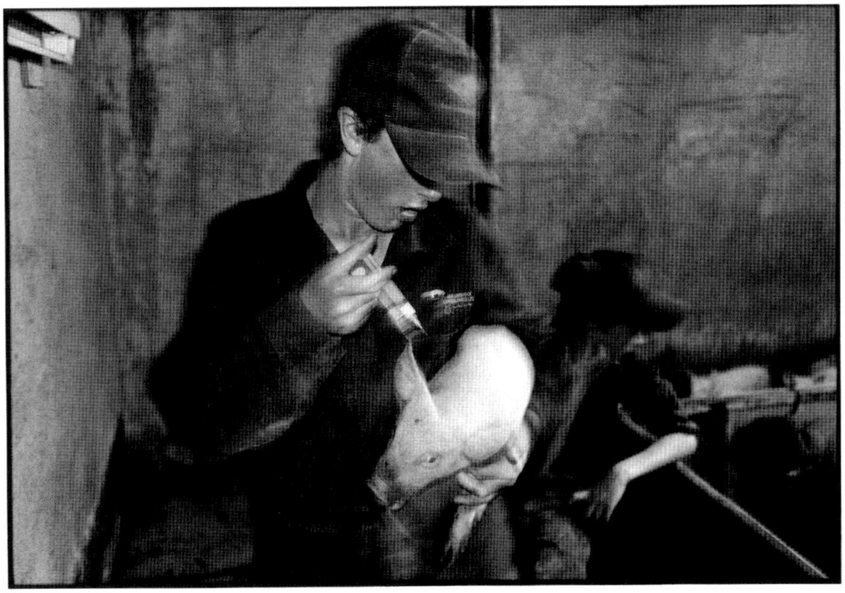

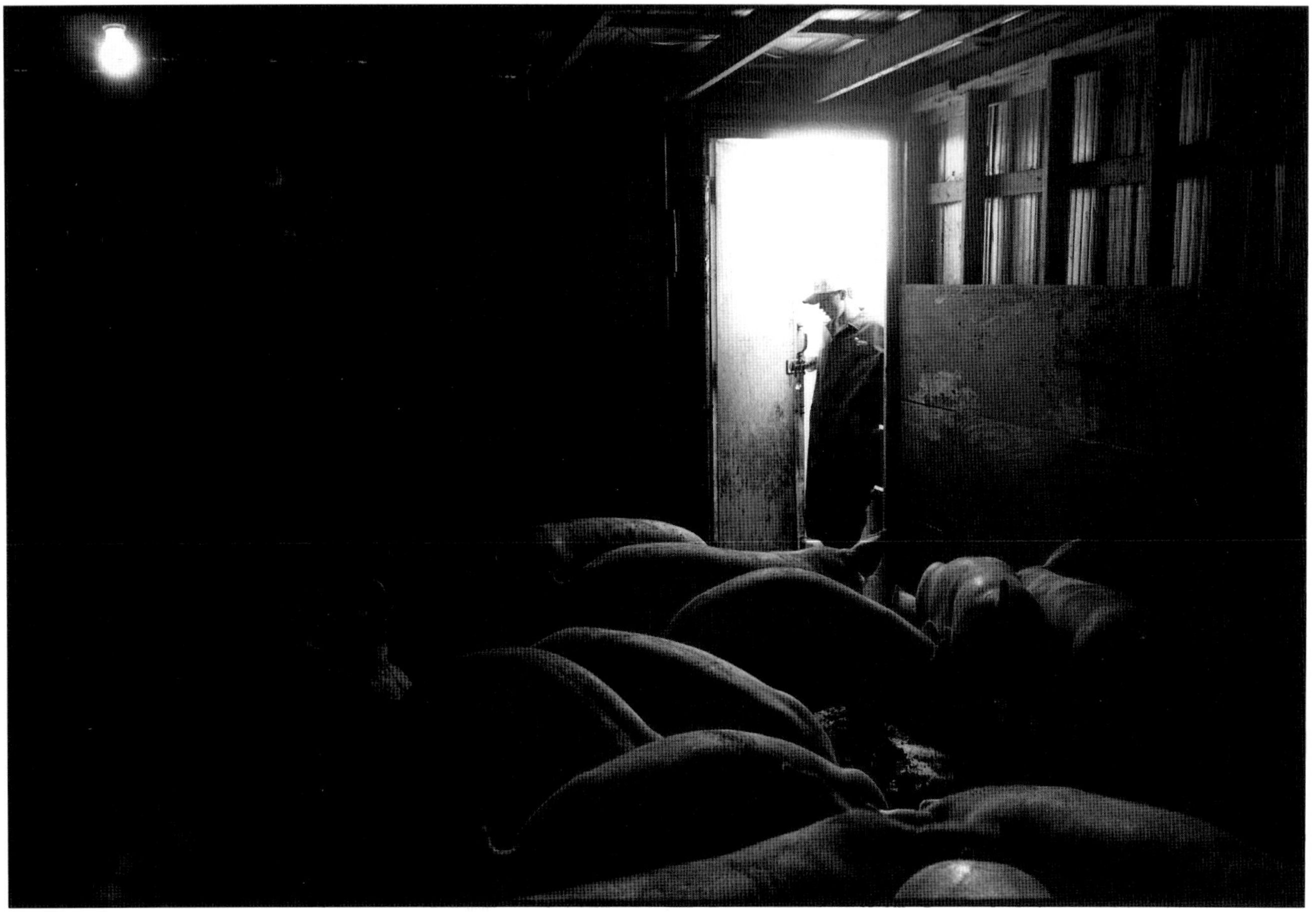

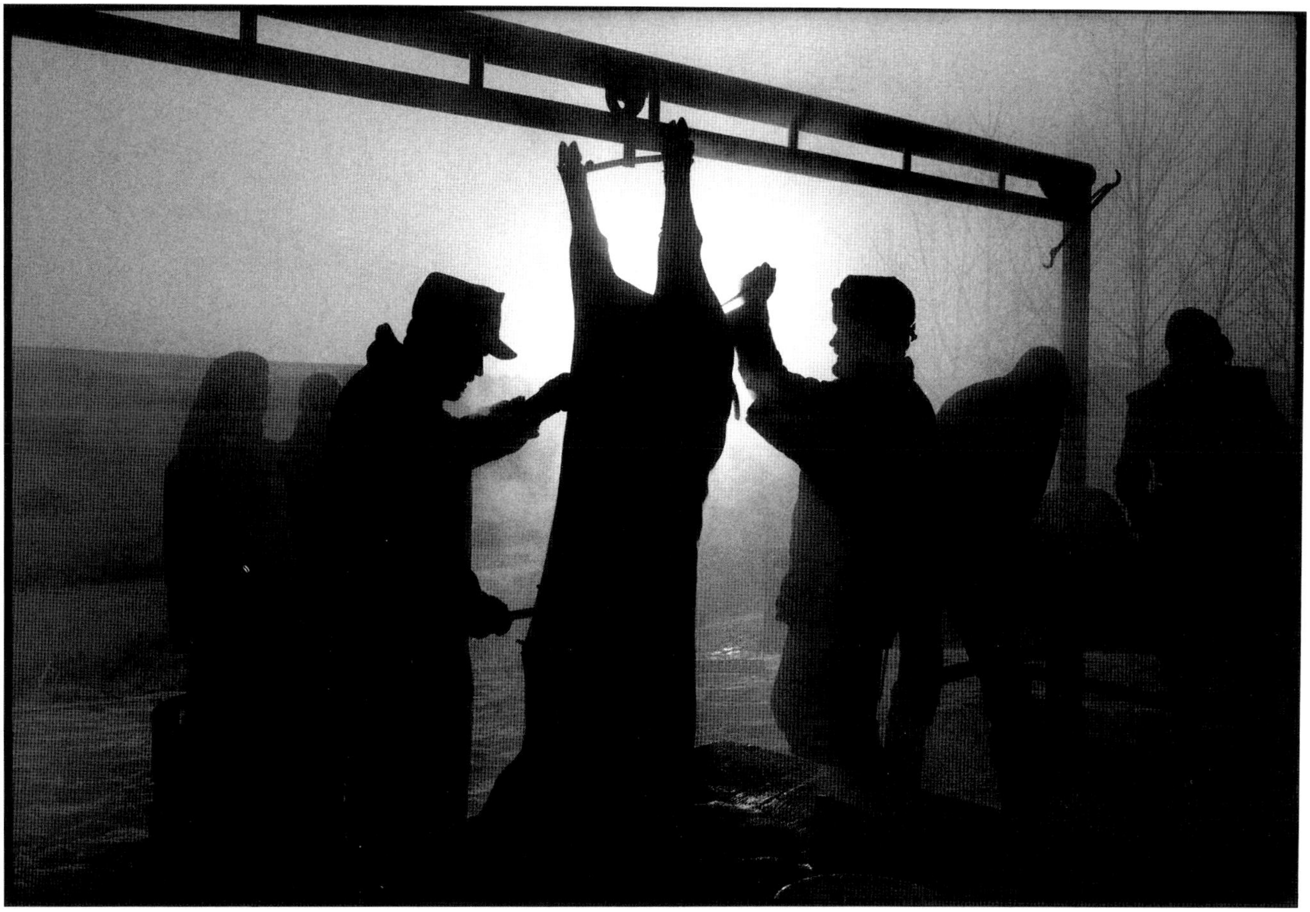

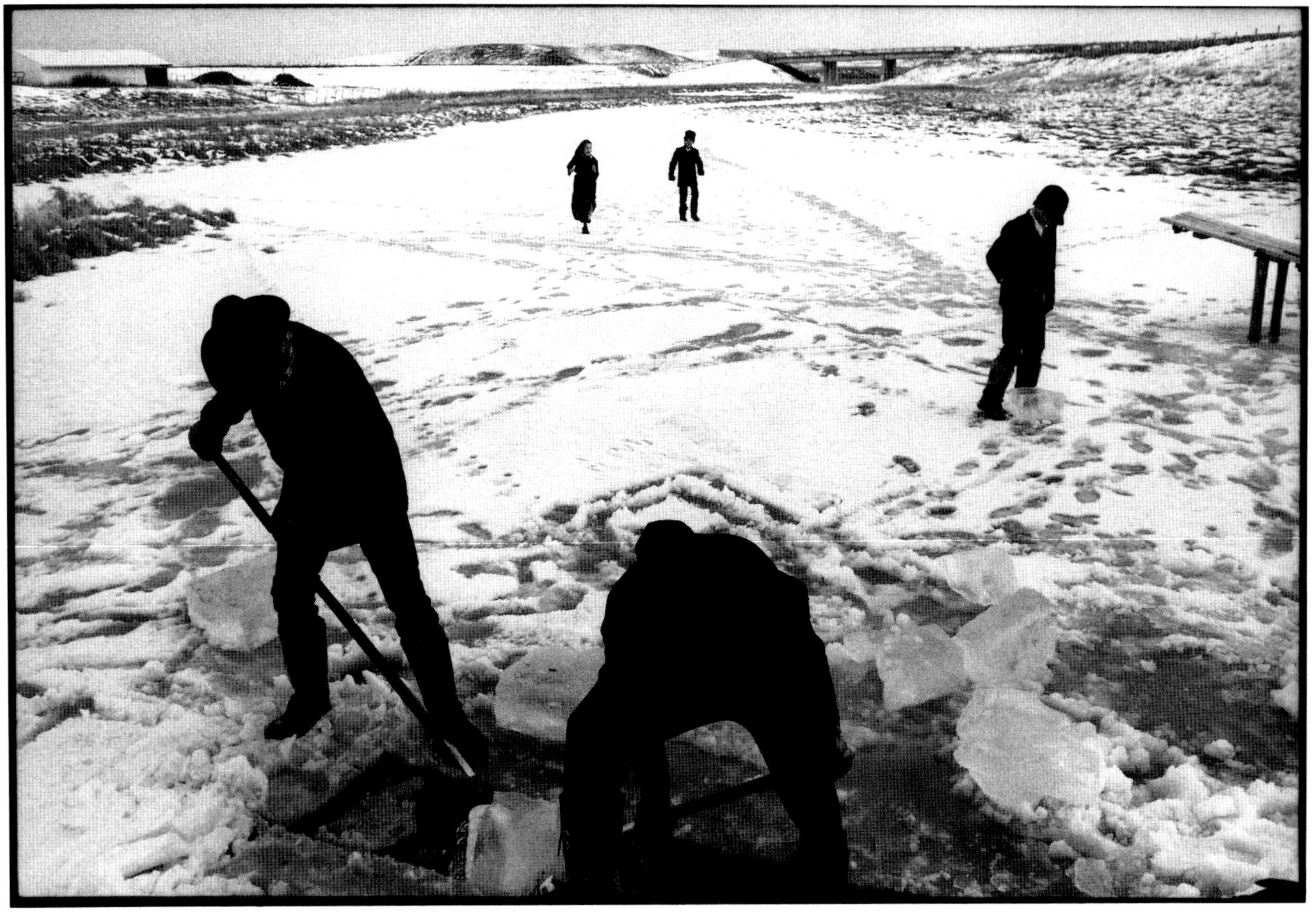

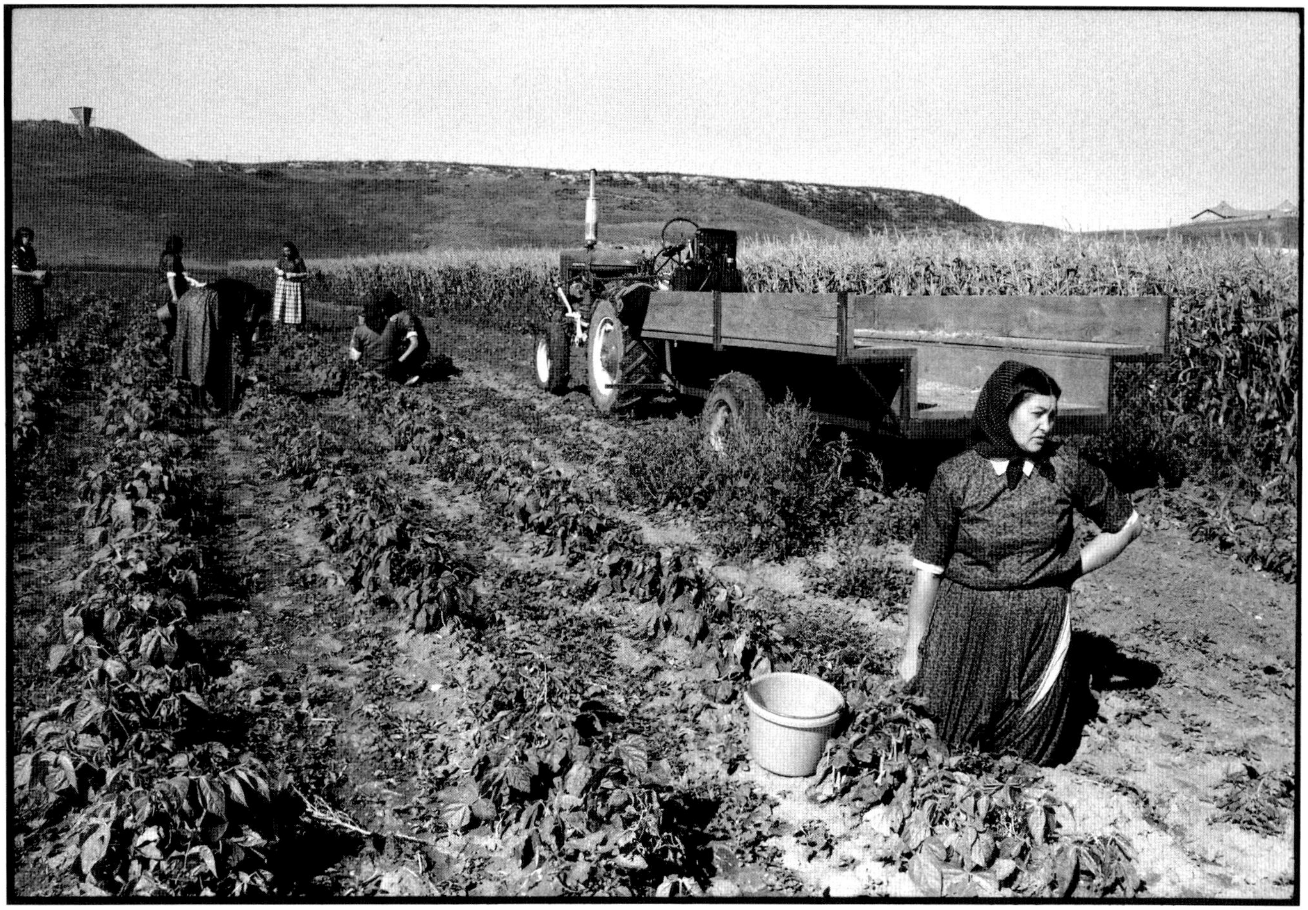

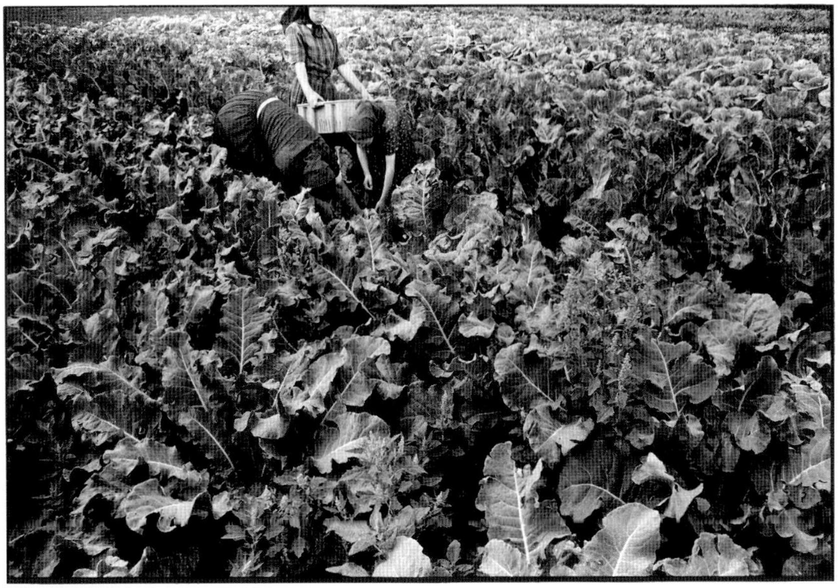

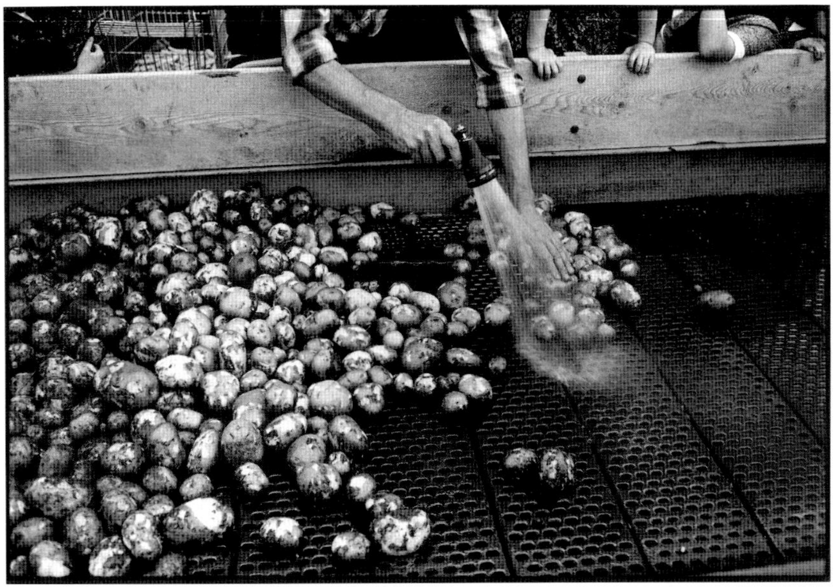

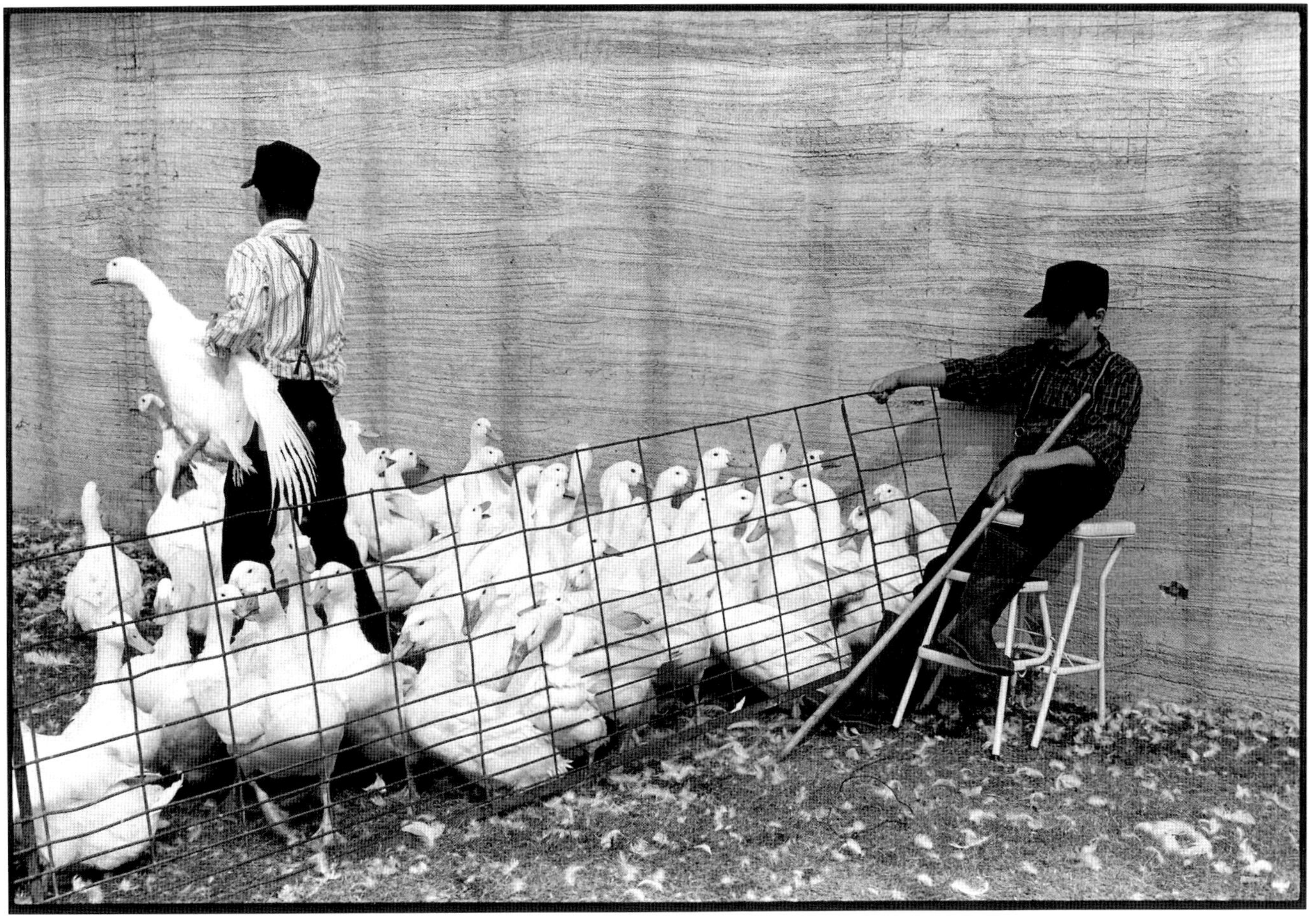

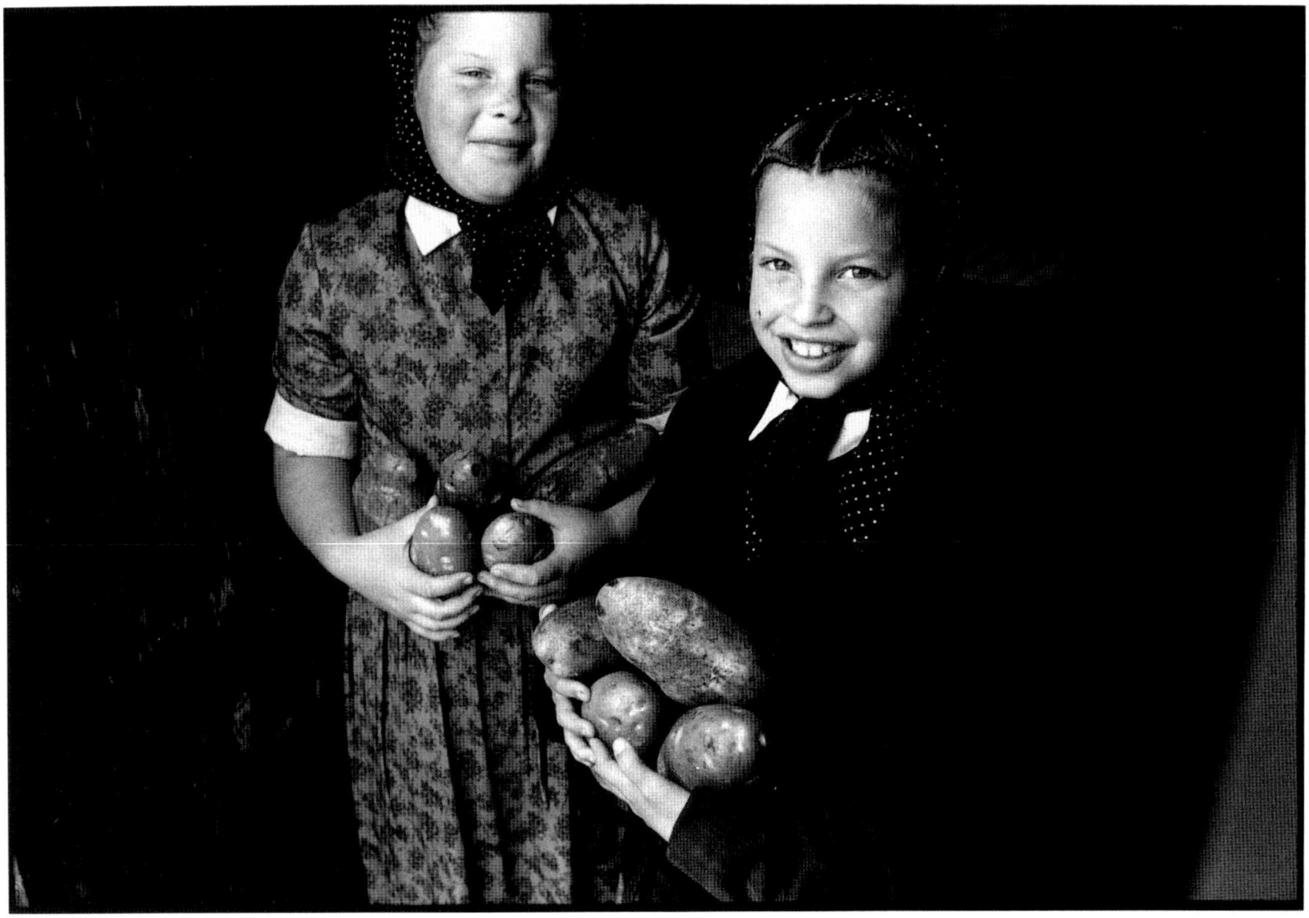

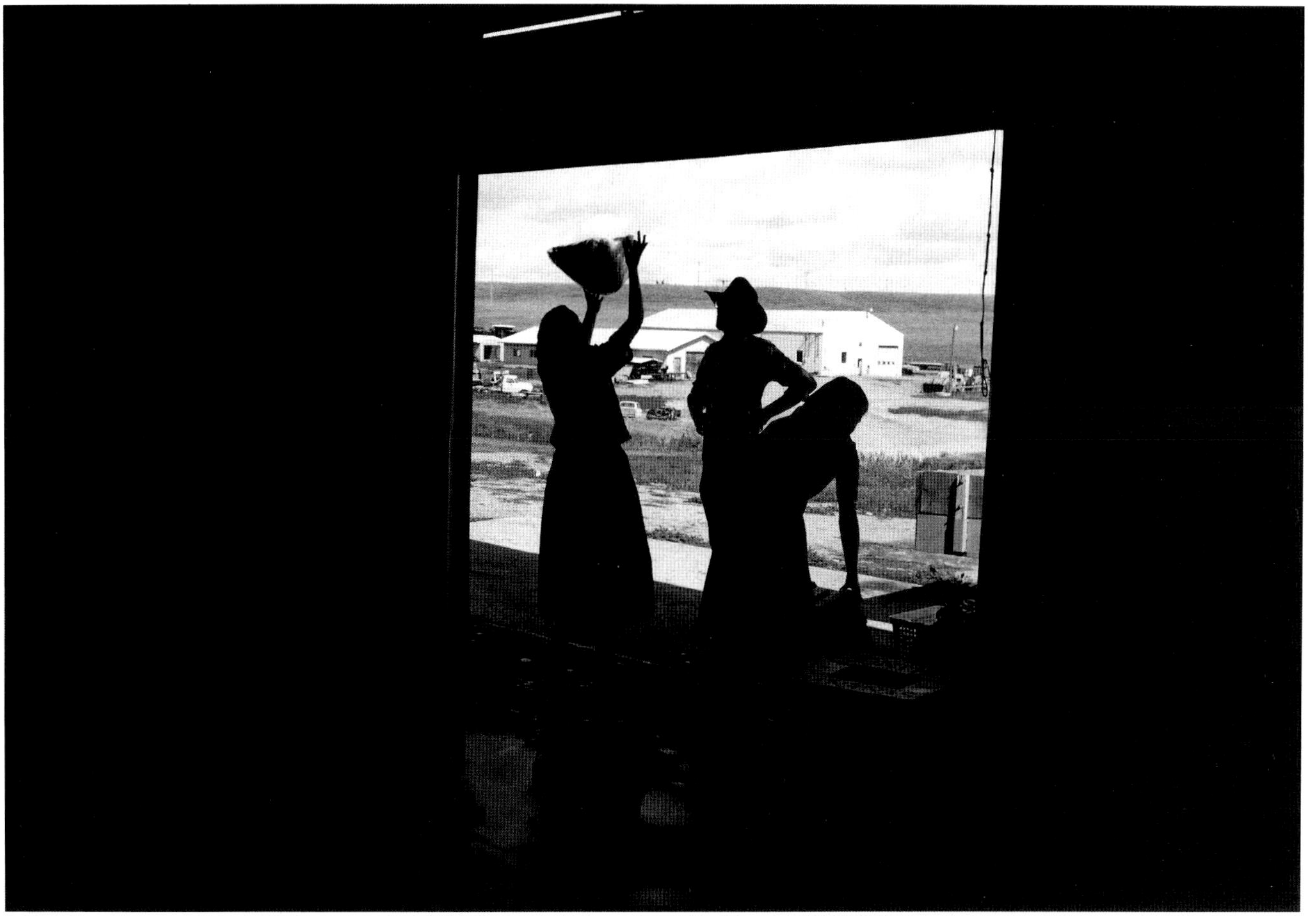

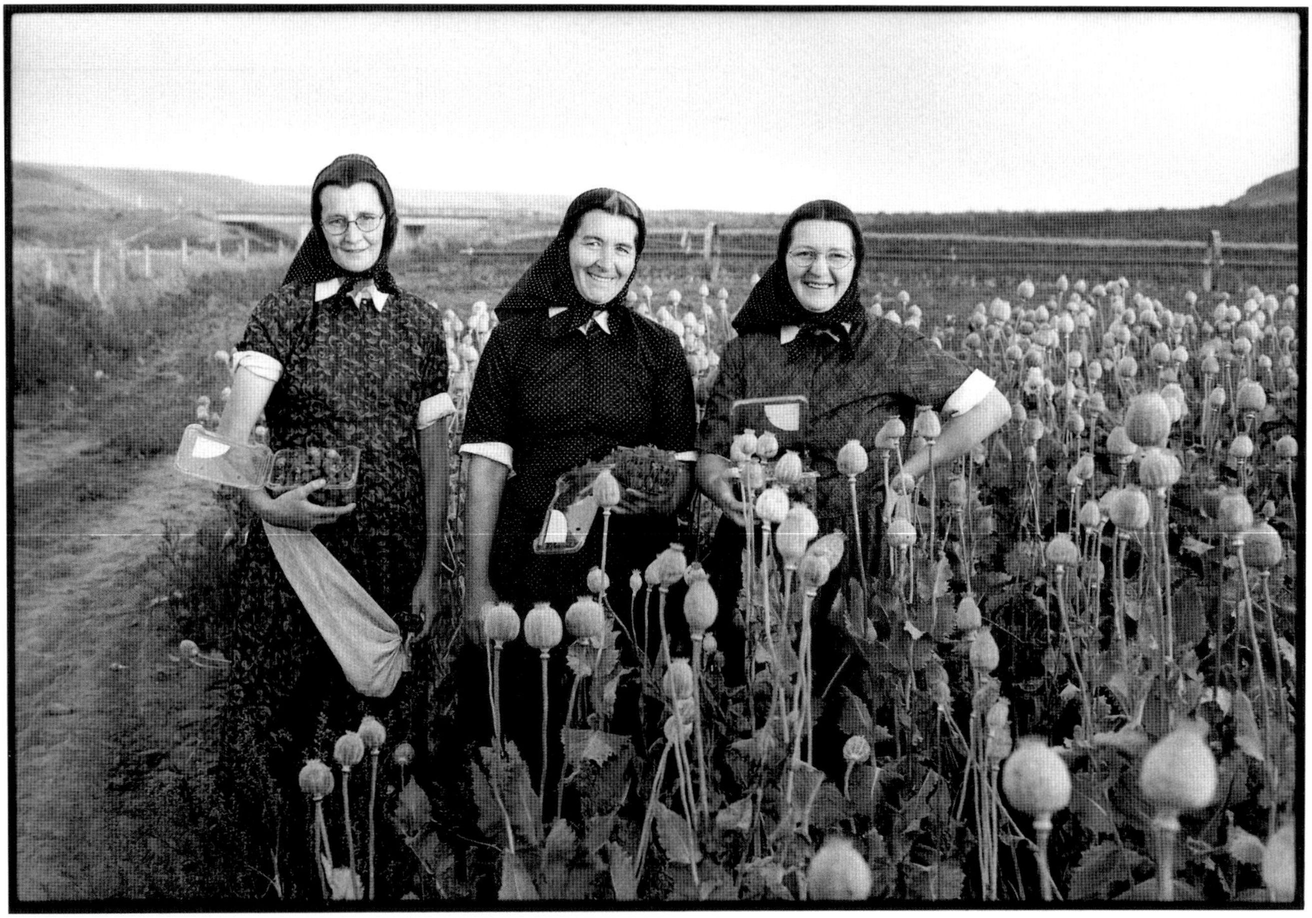

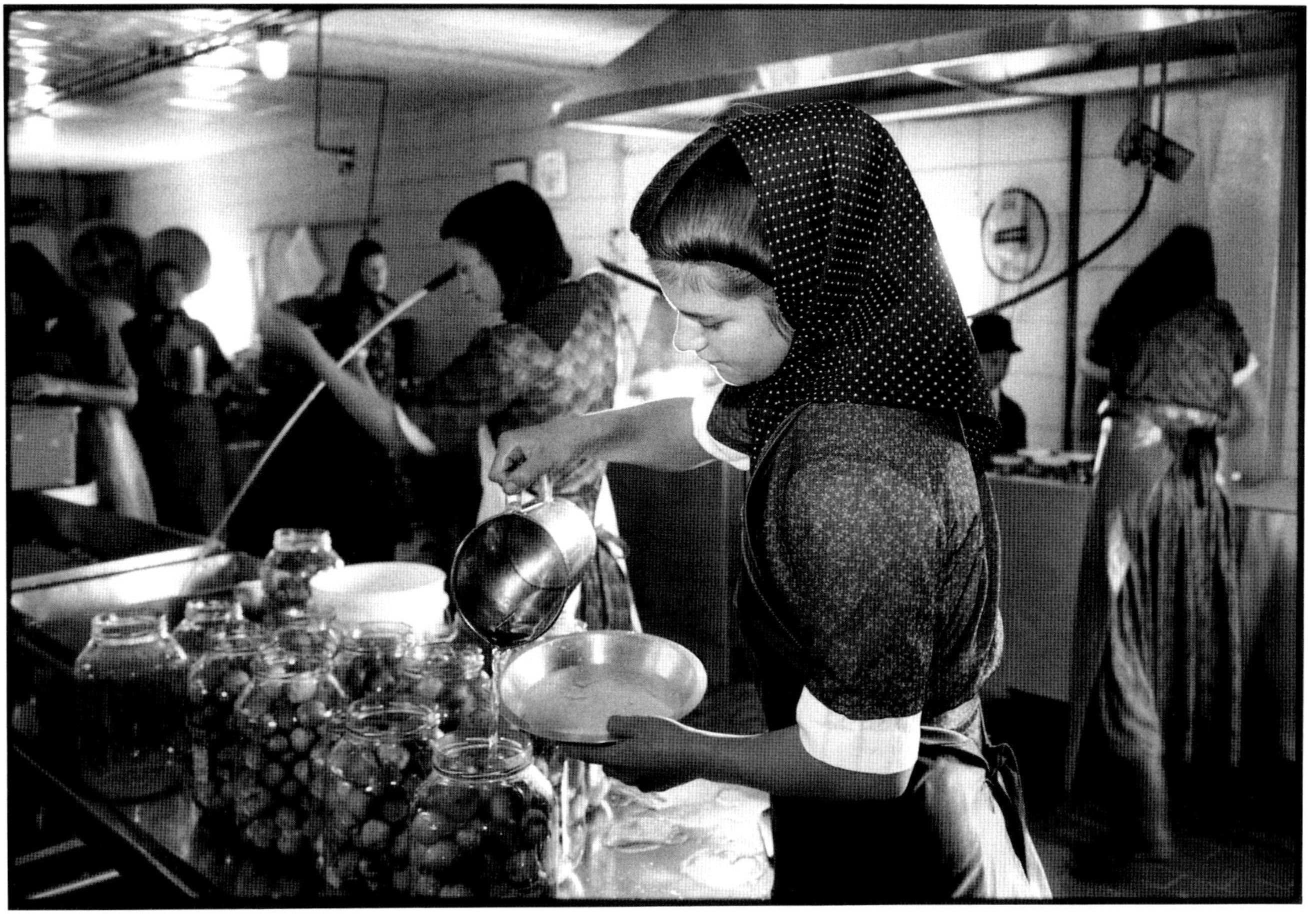

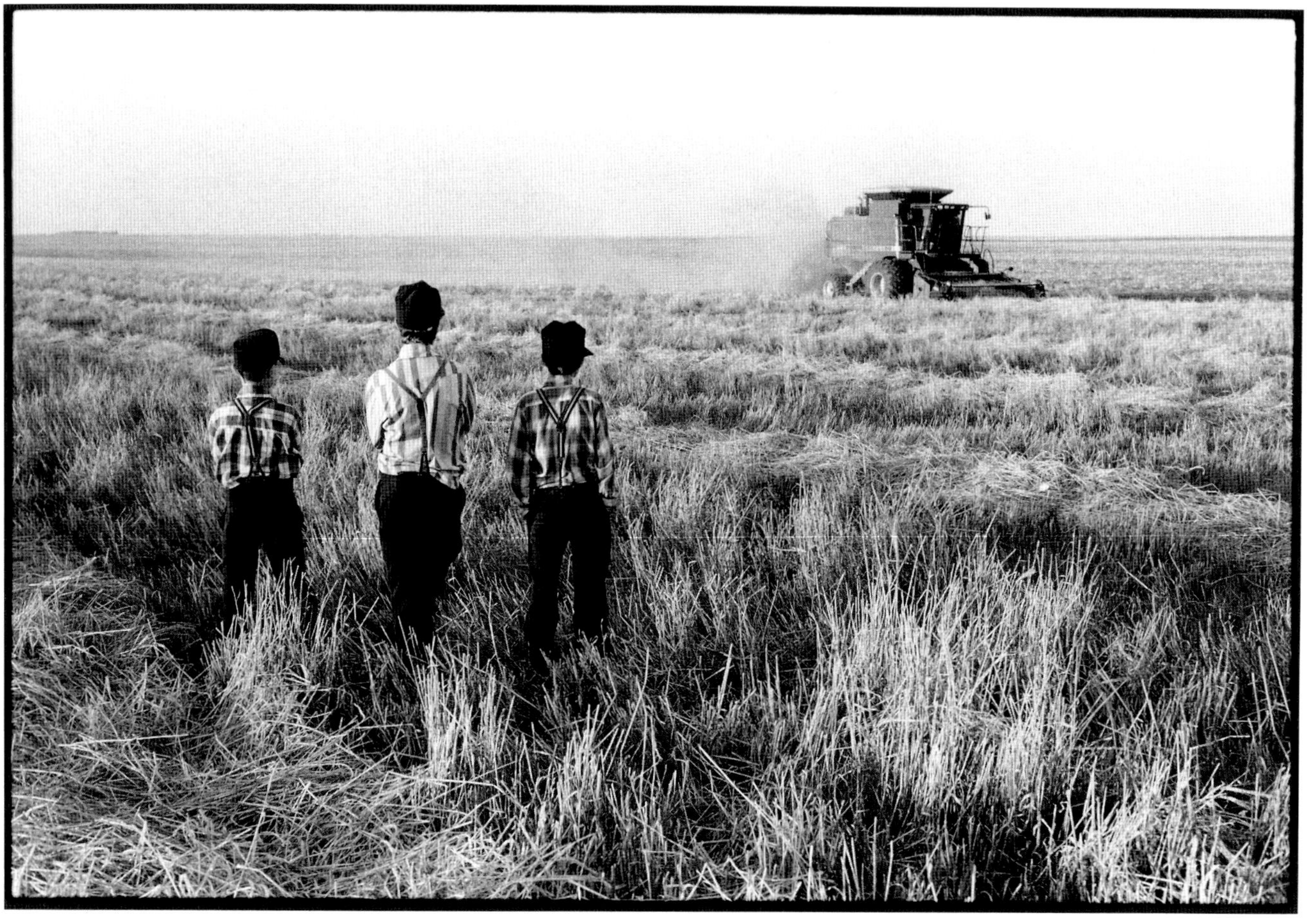

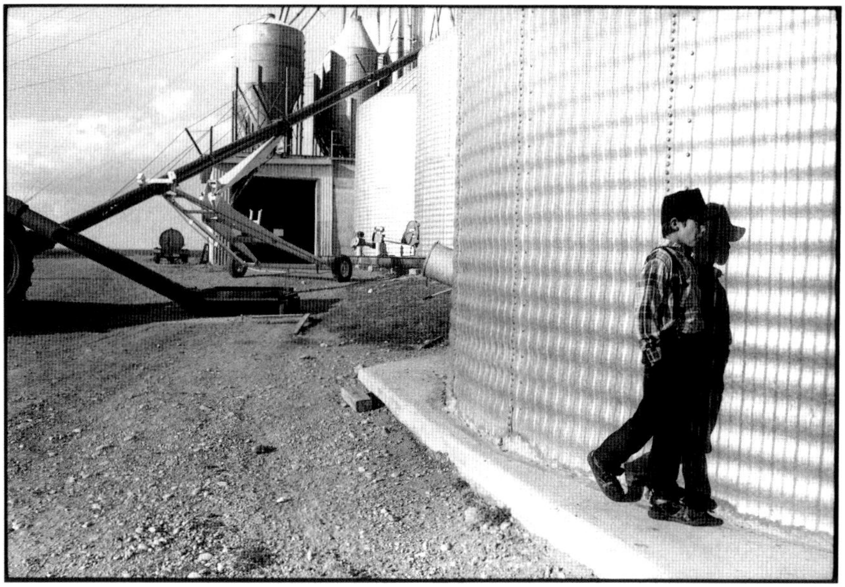

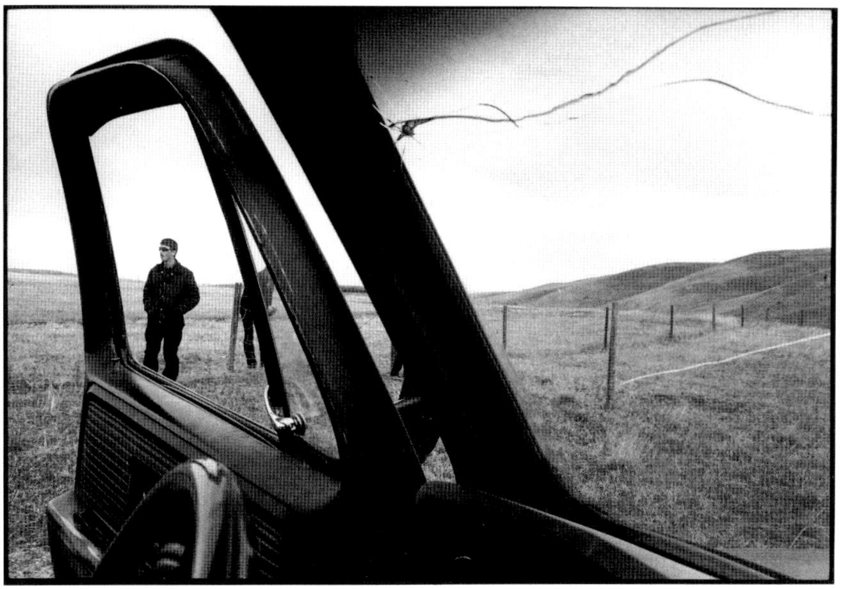

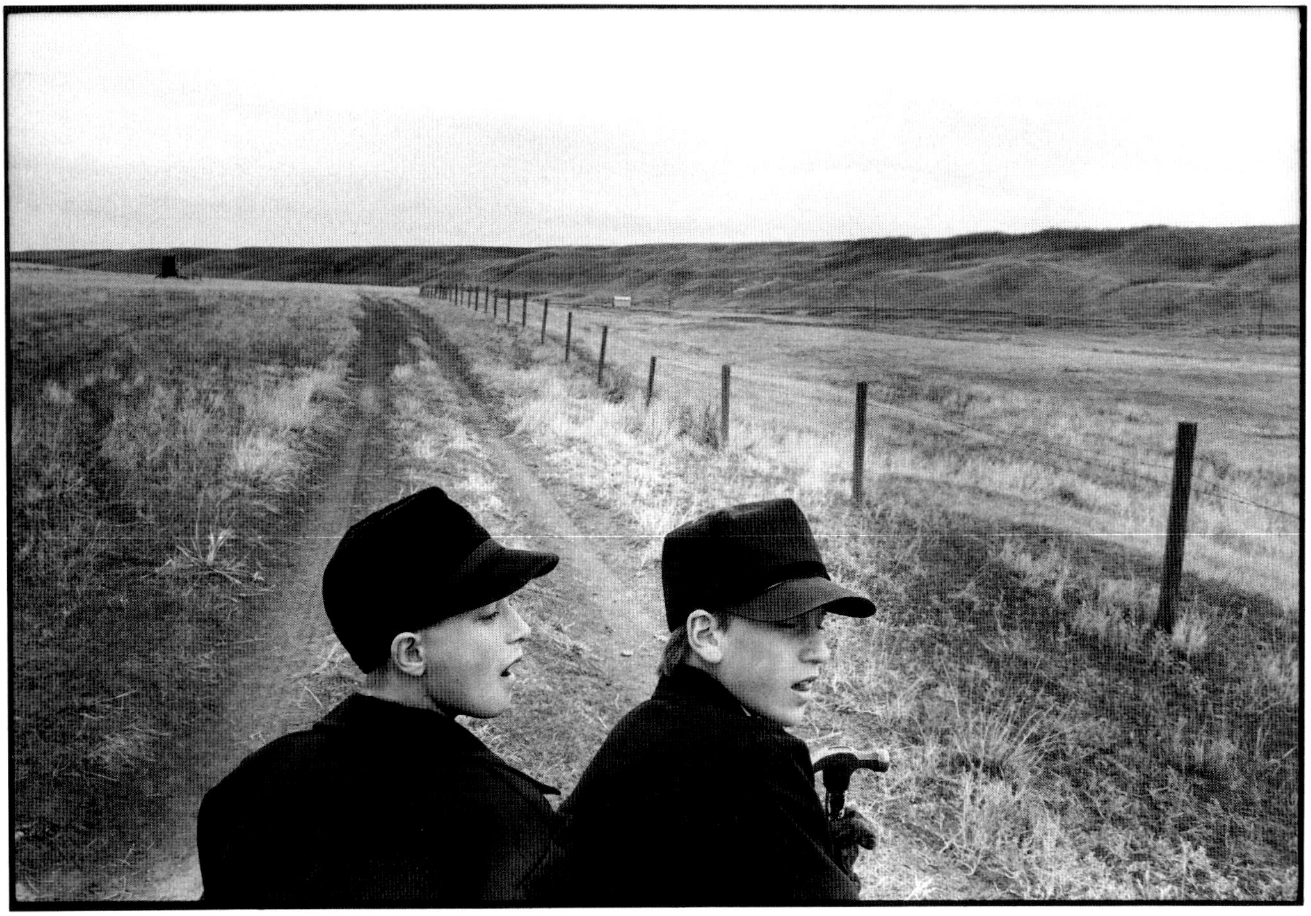

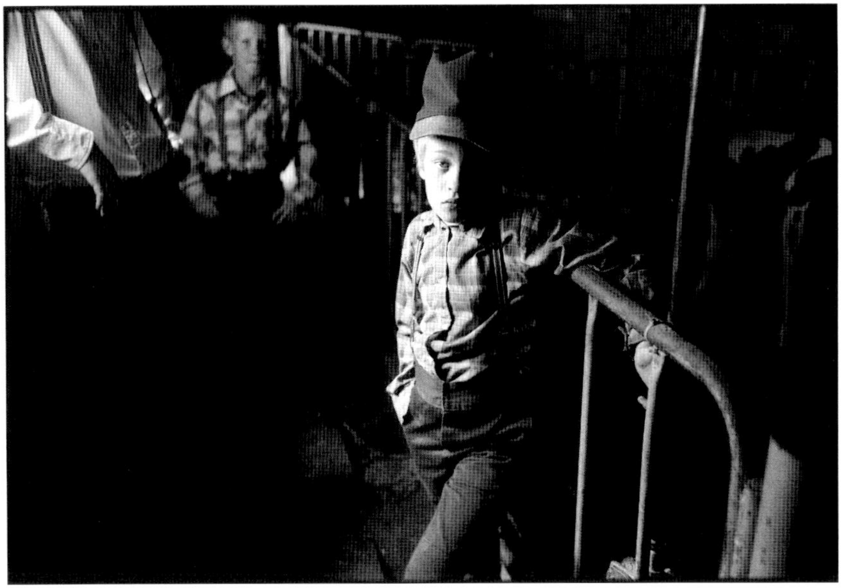

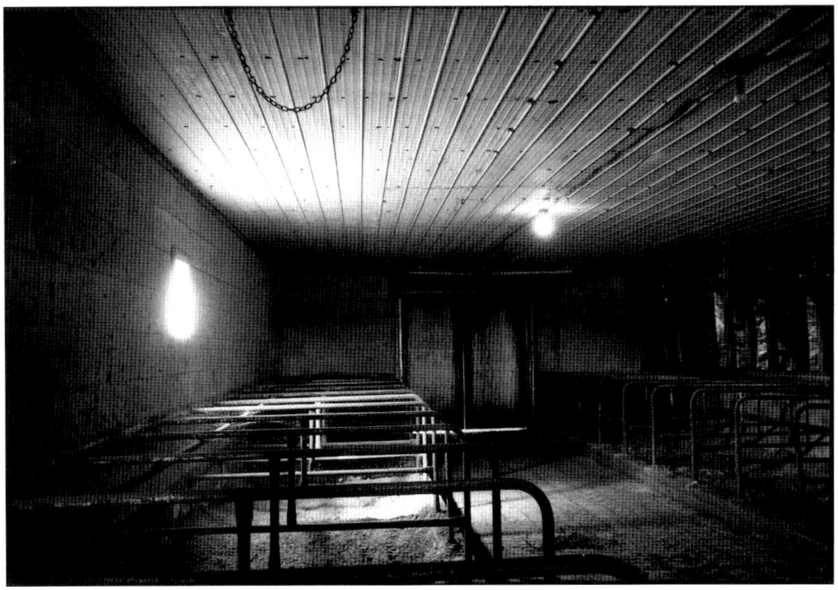

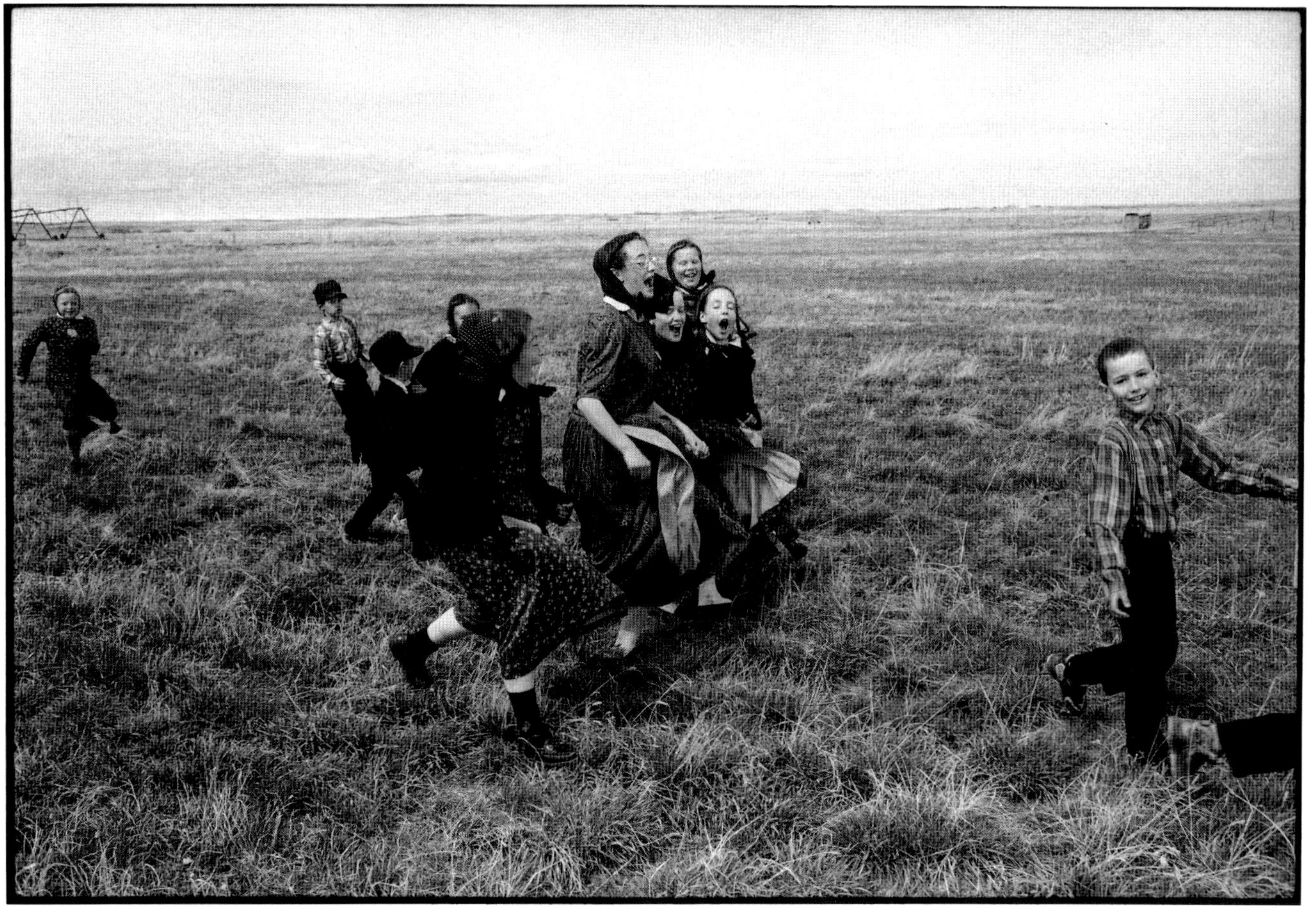

WE WILL REJOICE AND BE GLAD

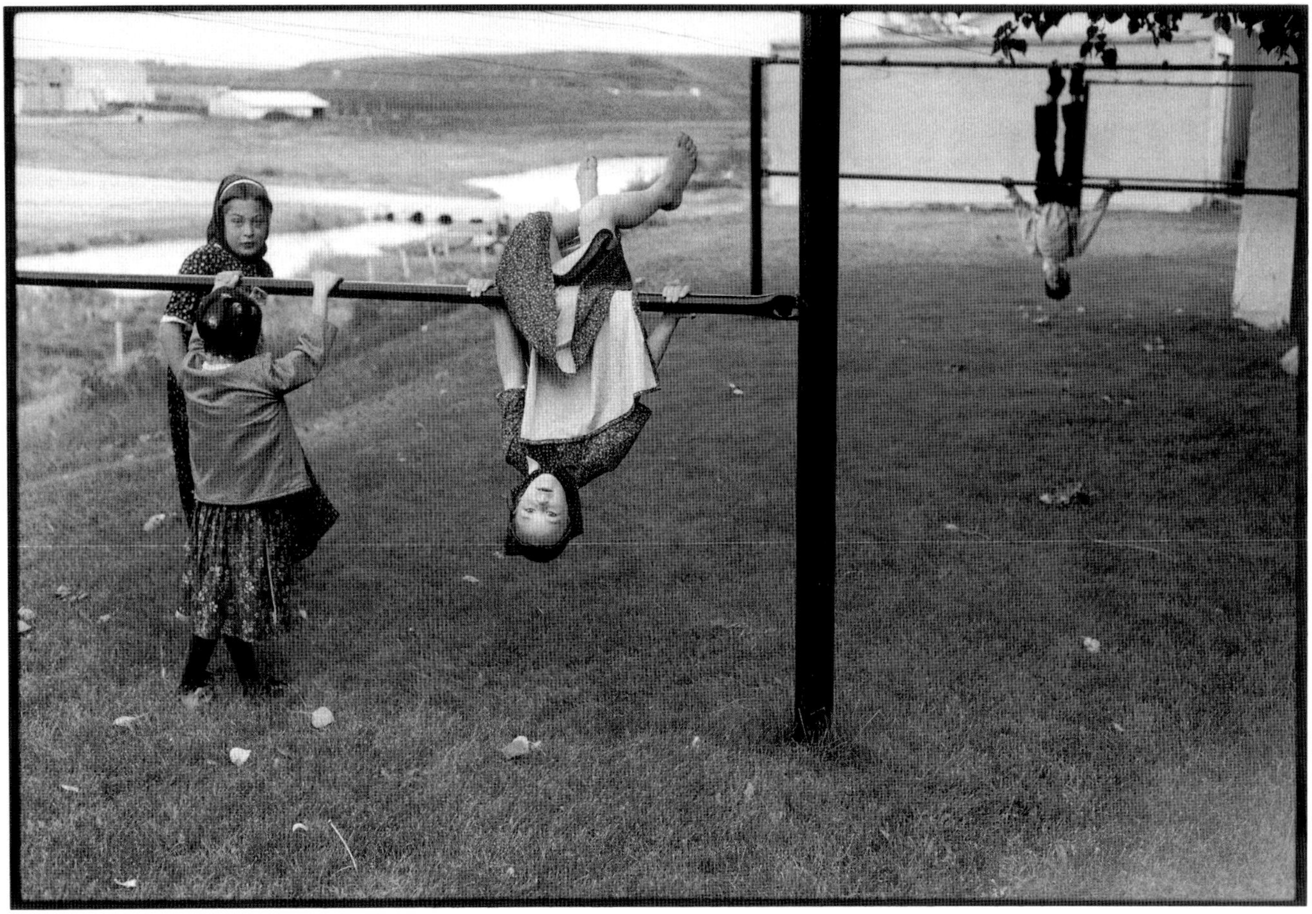

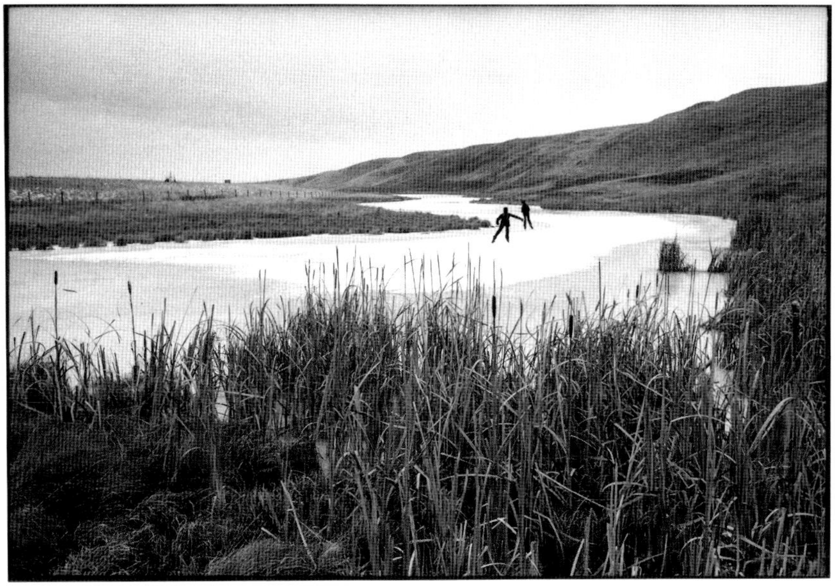

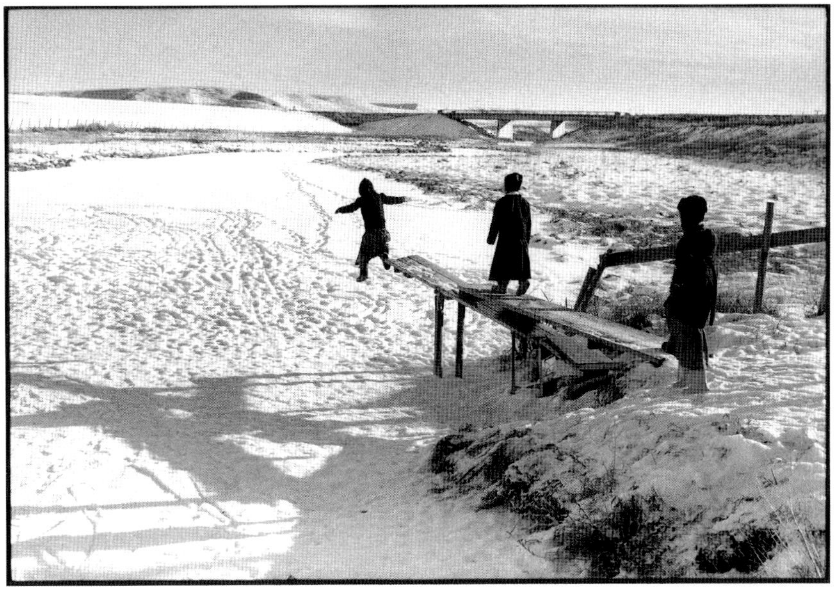

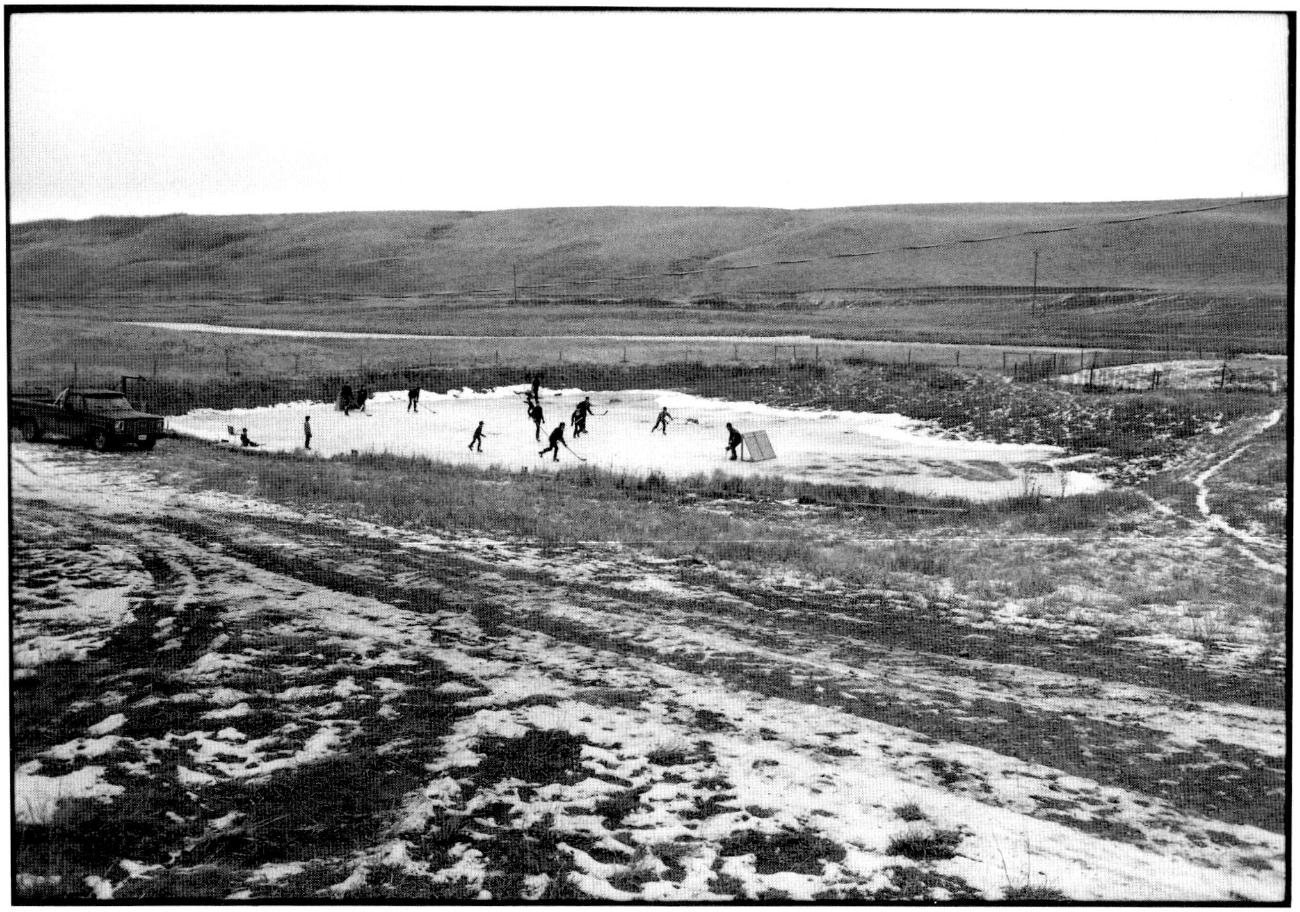

JUNE 20, 1999

"Garge! Garge! Garge!" chant the five girls on the kindergarten swings (then more words in German that I can't understand). One of their mothers, Katie, translates, "They're calling you Uncle George."

NOVEMBER 1999

The children are eager to show me their new kittens. They have made "homes" for them out of boxes and bits of insulation. Some of the kittens are dressed in doll clothes. Many of these kittens come from mother cats who were abandoned near the colony.

DECEMBER 15, 1999

The pick-up hockey game on the frozen auxiliary sewage pond.

Sliding along the beautiful dark ice of the frozen Little Bow River with the boys.

JANUARY 28, 2000

Sledding with the kids from the top of the colony down to the frozen river.

After supper Mathew tells me he has something for me and takes me to his house and gives me a big bag of Christmas candy. Old Joe puts a bag of carrots and potatoes in my truck, and Katie packs a big bag of "goodies" consisting of buns, crackers, chocolate, and cherries.

AUGUST 14, 2000

Paul has been chosen to be the new minister of the colony.

A yellow-striped garter snake appears at the swimming hole … squeals of terror as the kids quickly seek the safety of the shore.

APRIL 13, 2001
(GOOD FRIDAY)

One of the young colony girls, Marilyn, prints her name on the dust of my rear windshield.

DECEMBER 26, 2001

I bring my skates and go down to the frozen river with four of the girls. Maria and Marilyn have old black hockey skates, probably inherited from their brothers. The girls hadn't done much skating. They bounce and veer across the ice gleefully. Wendy and Sharon slide along the ice in their rubber boots, doing their best to keep up to the skaters. More kids join us and one of them devises an idea for a game. The children lie on their backs on the ice, the soles of their feet touching the head of the next person, forming a line of little bodies in toques and mittens. I am instructed to skate "way far back," then skate as fast as I can towards them, open my legs into an inverted "v," and skate right over top of them.

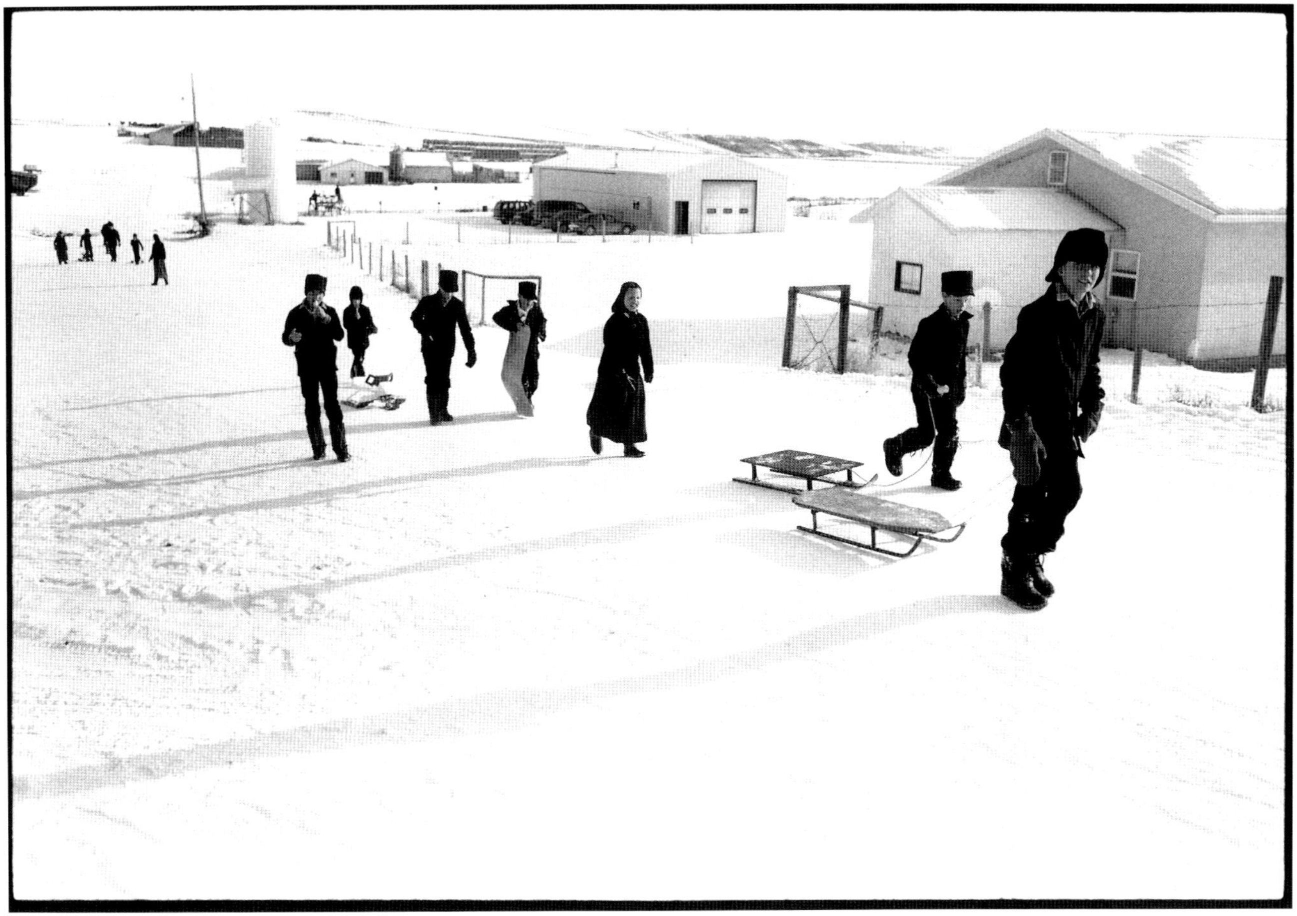

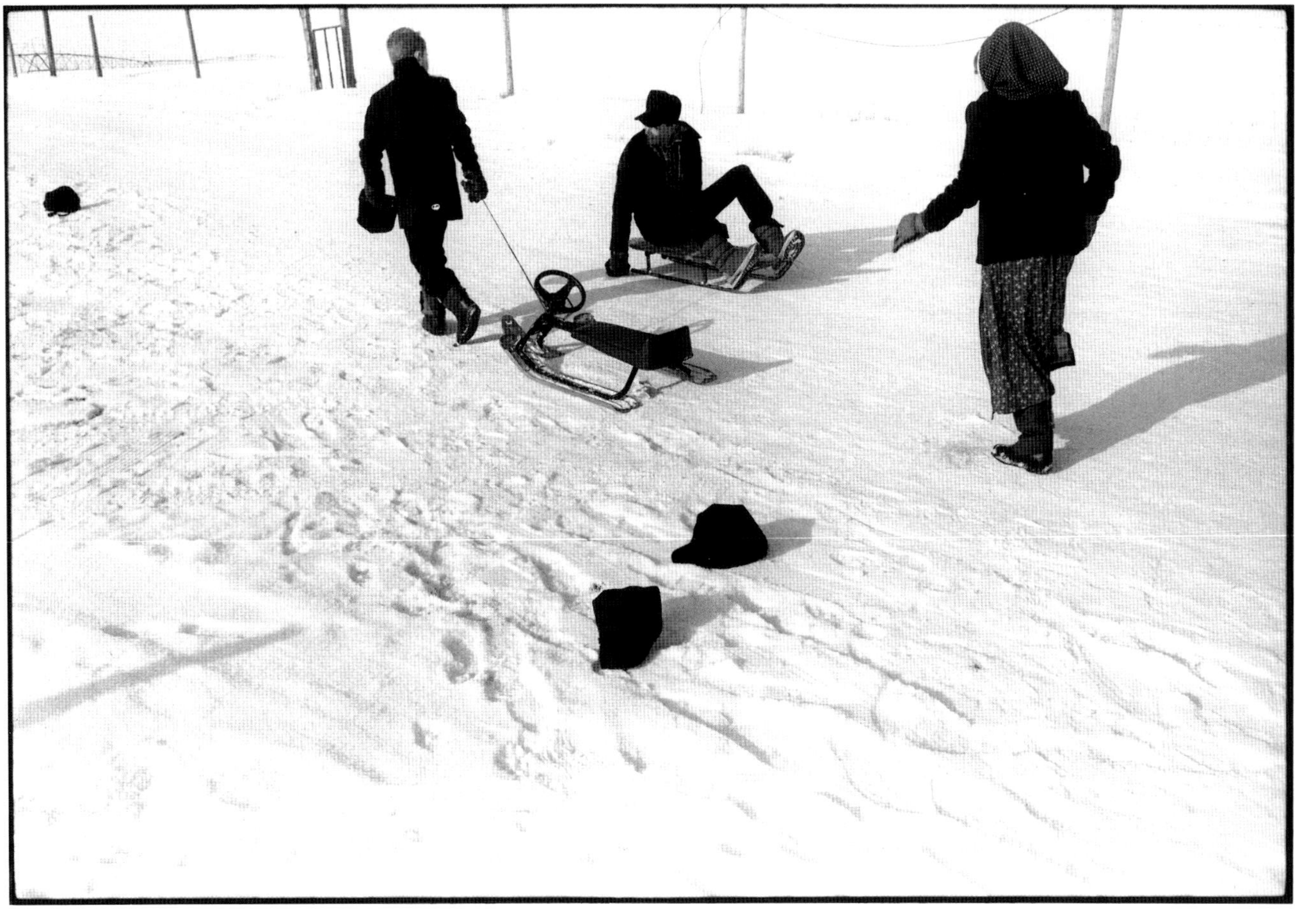

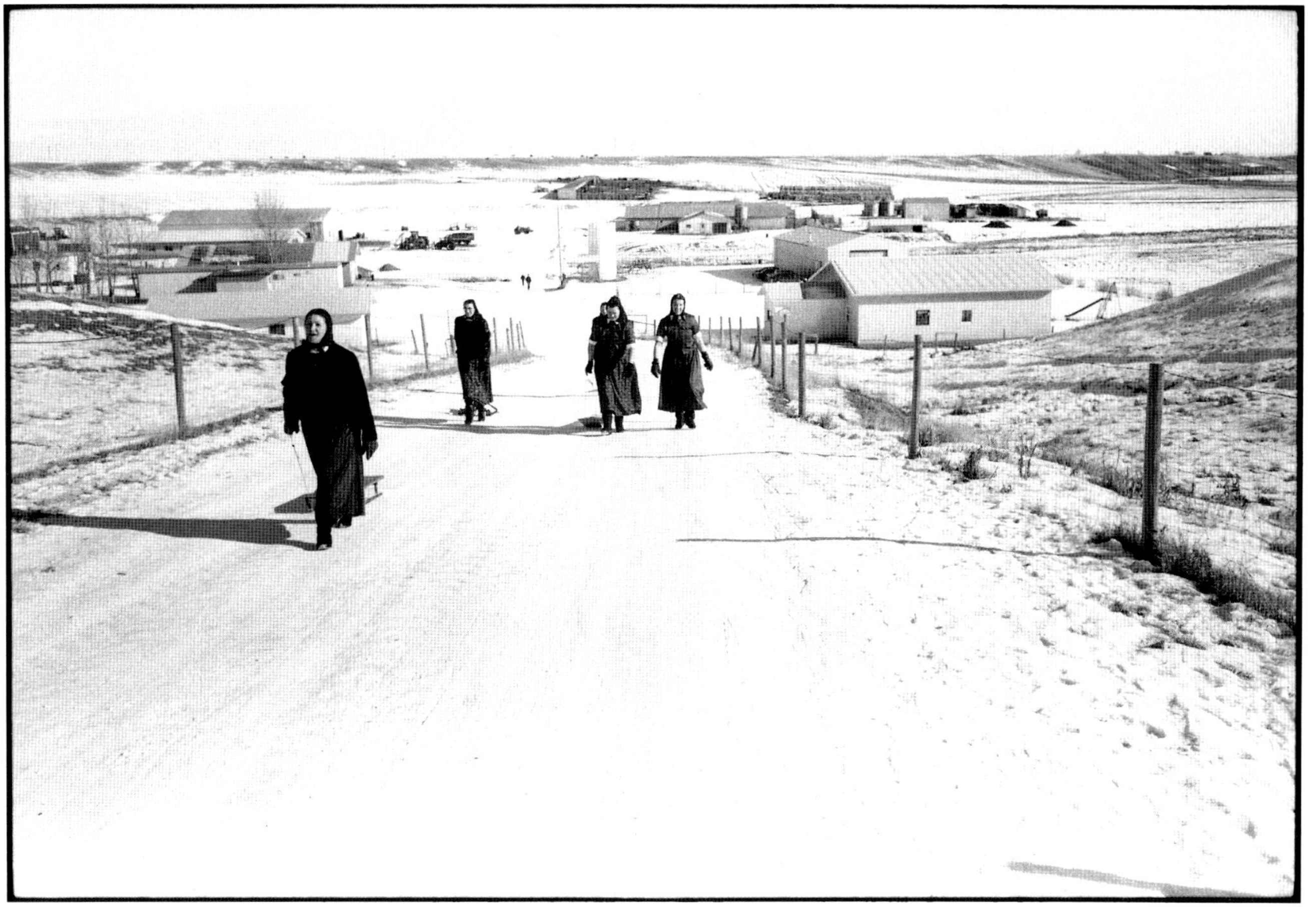

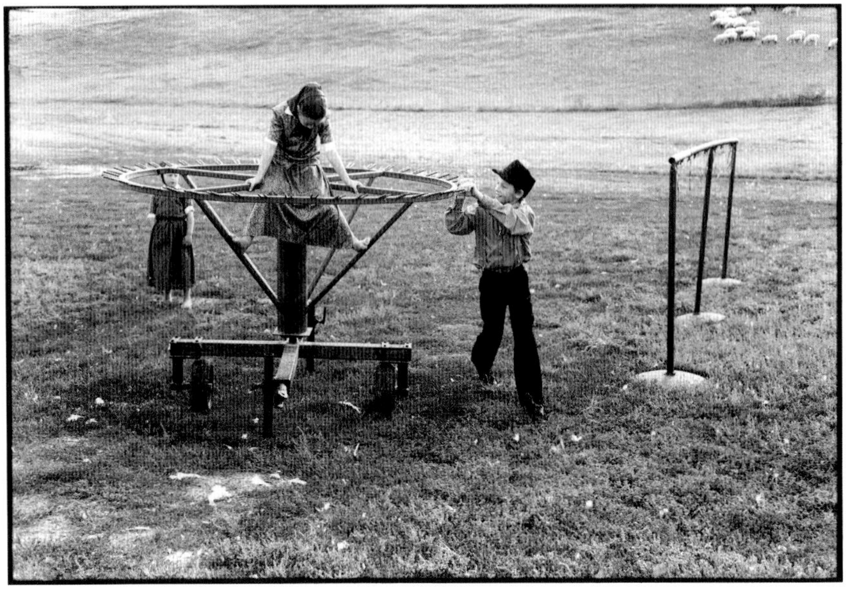

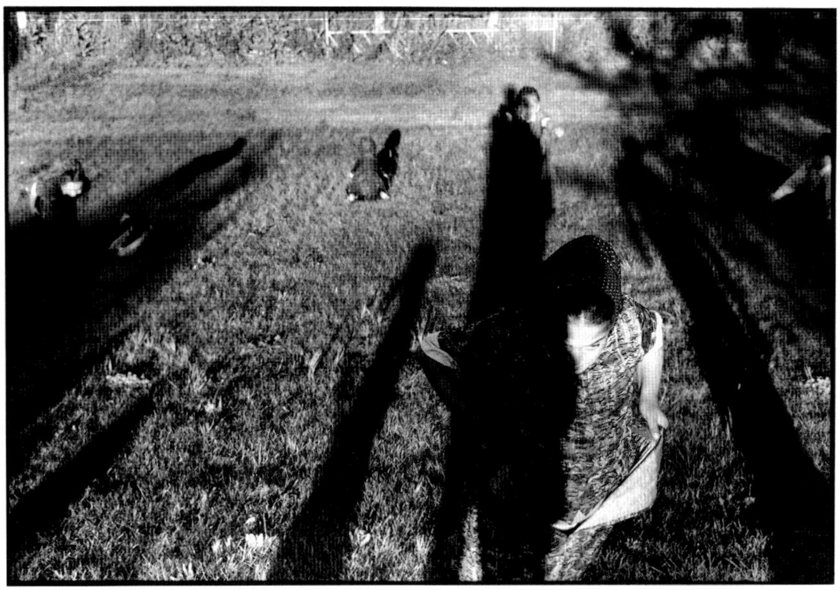

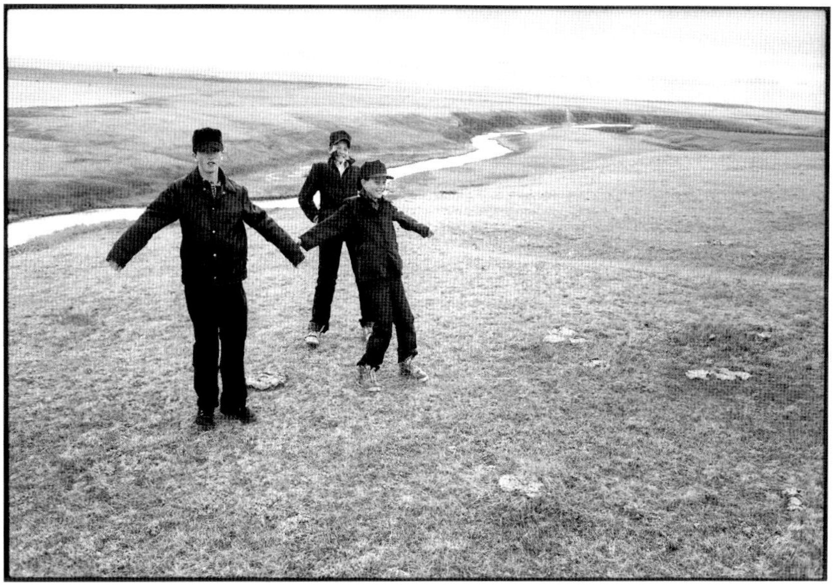

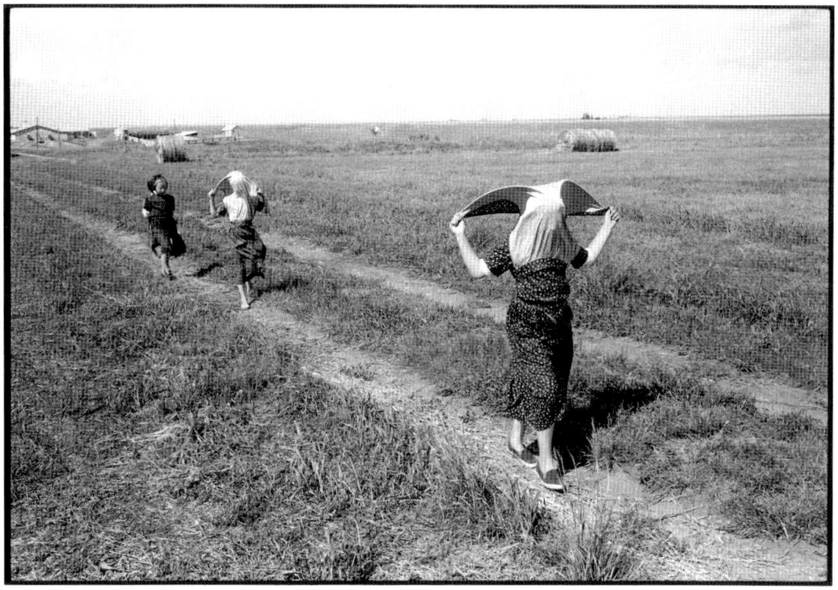

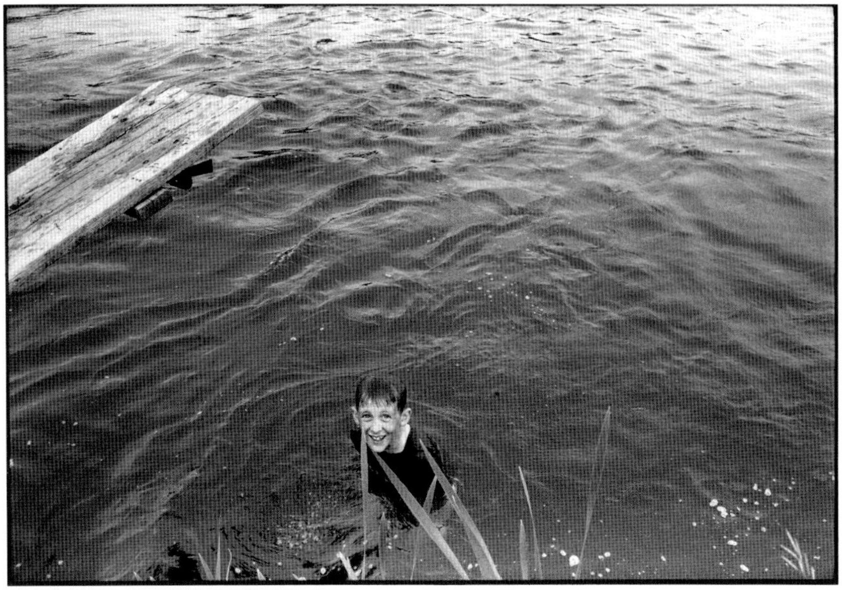

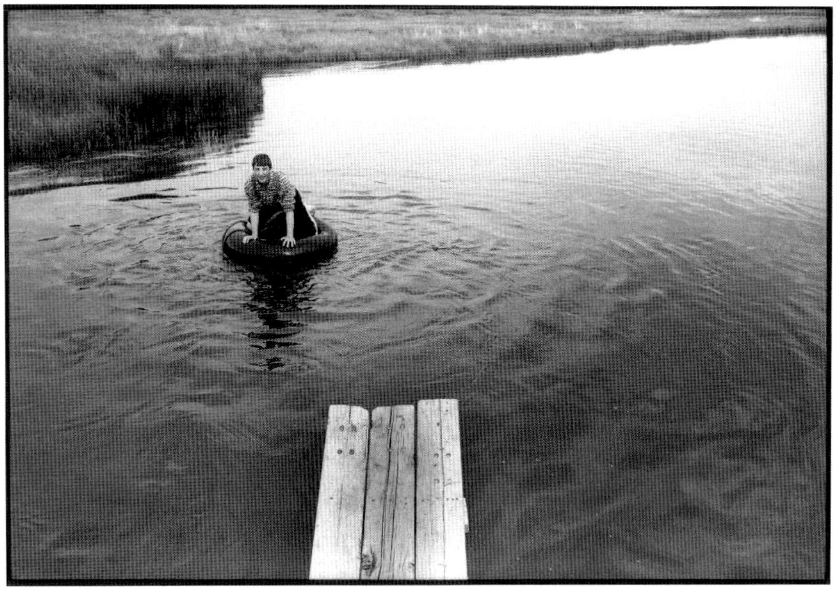

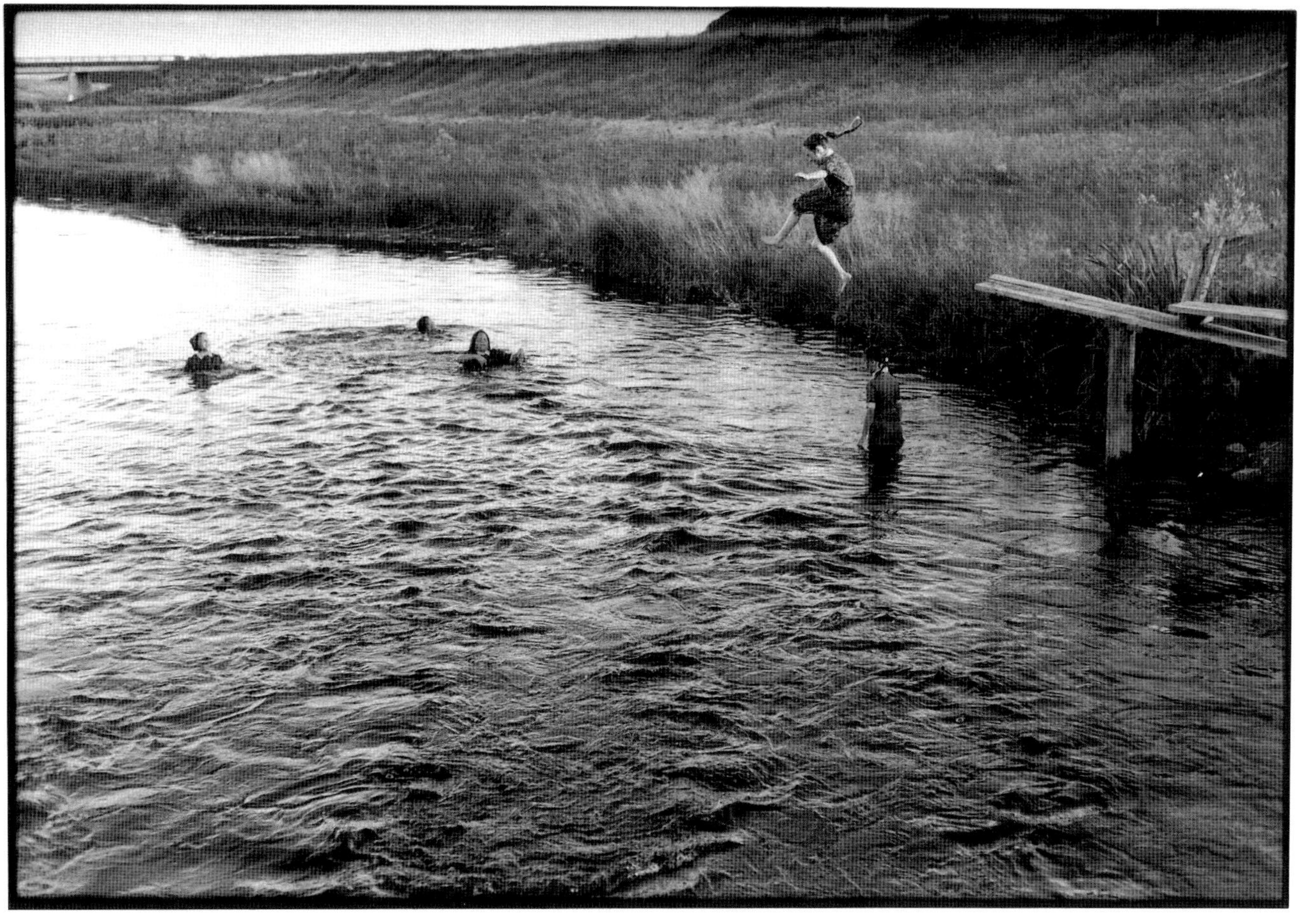

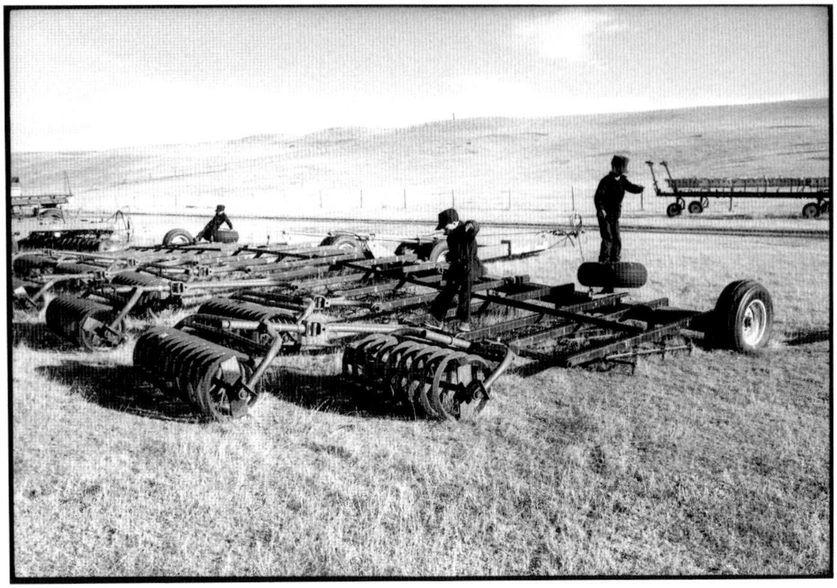

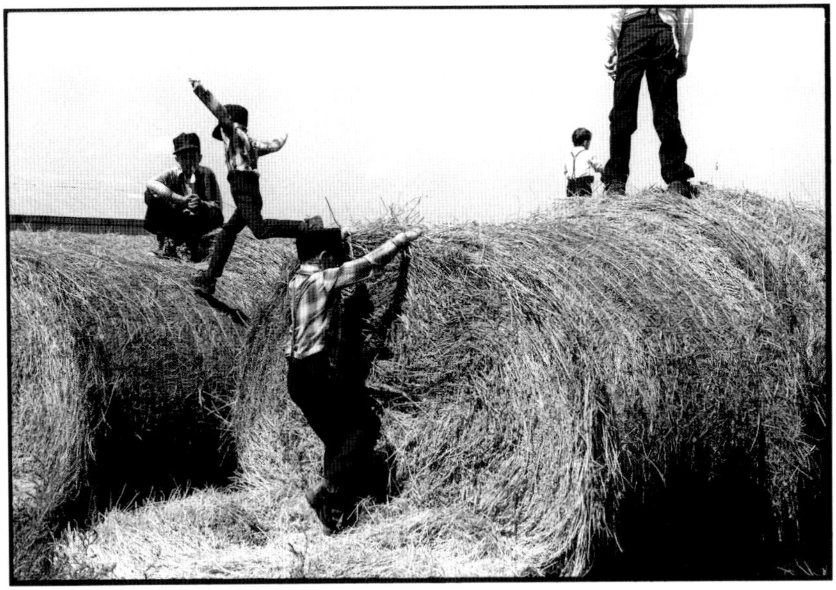

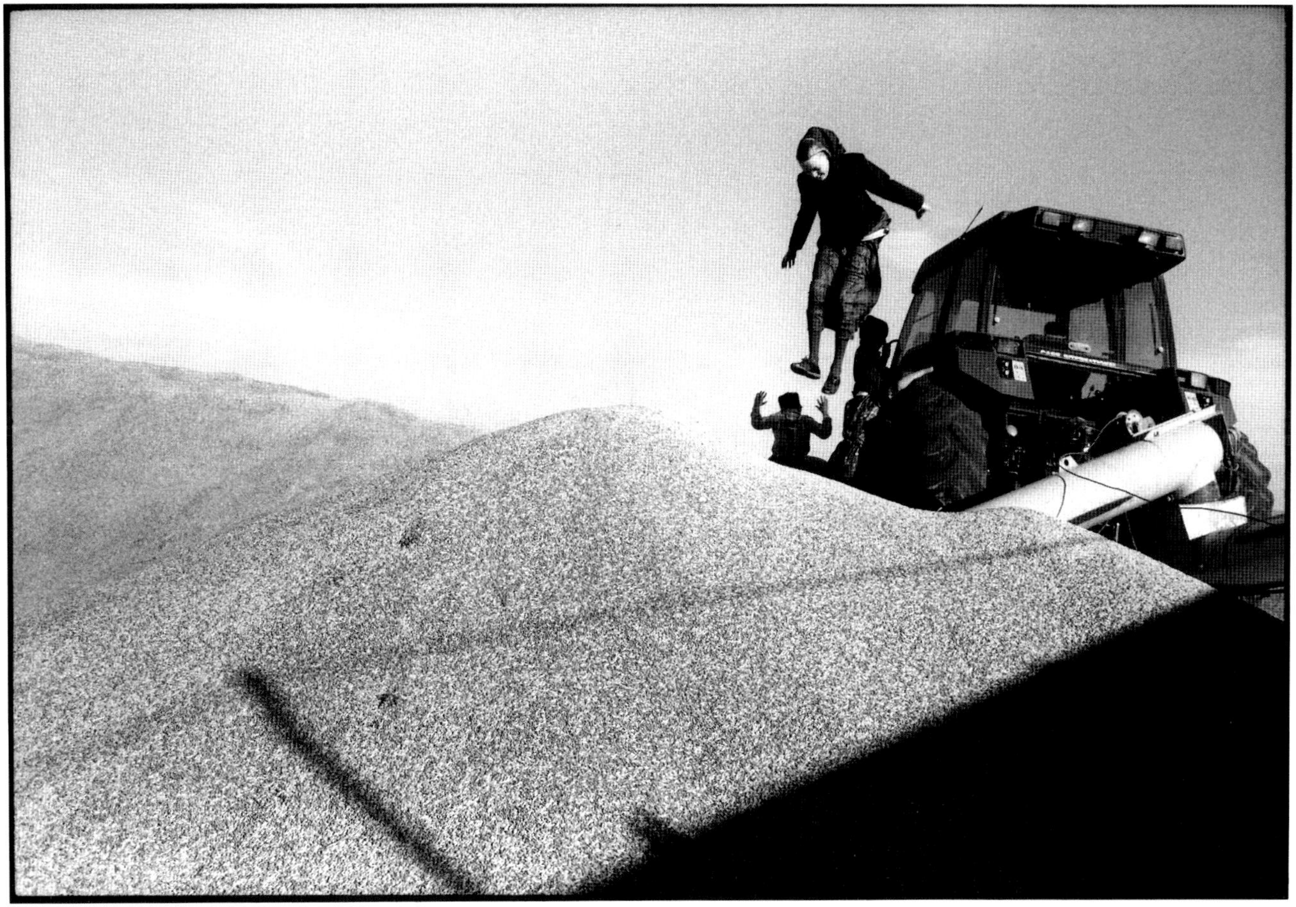

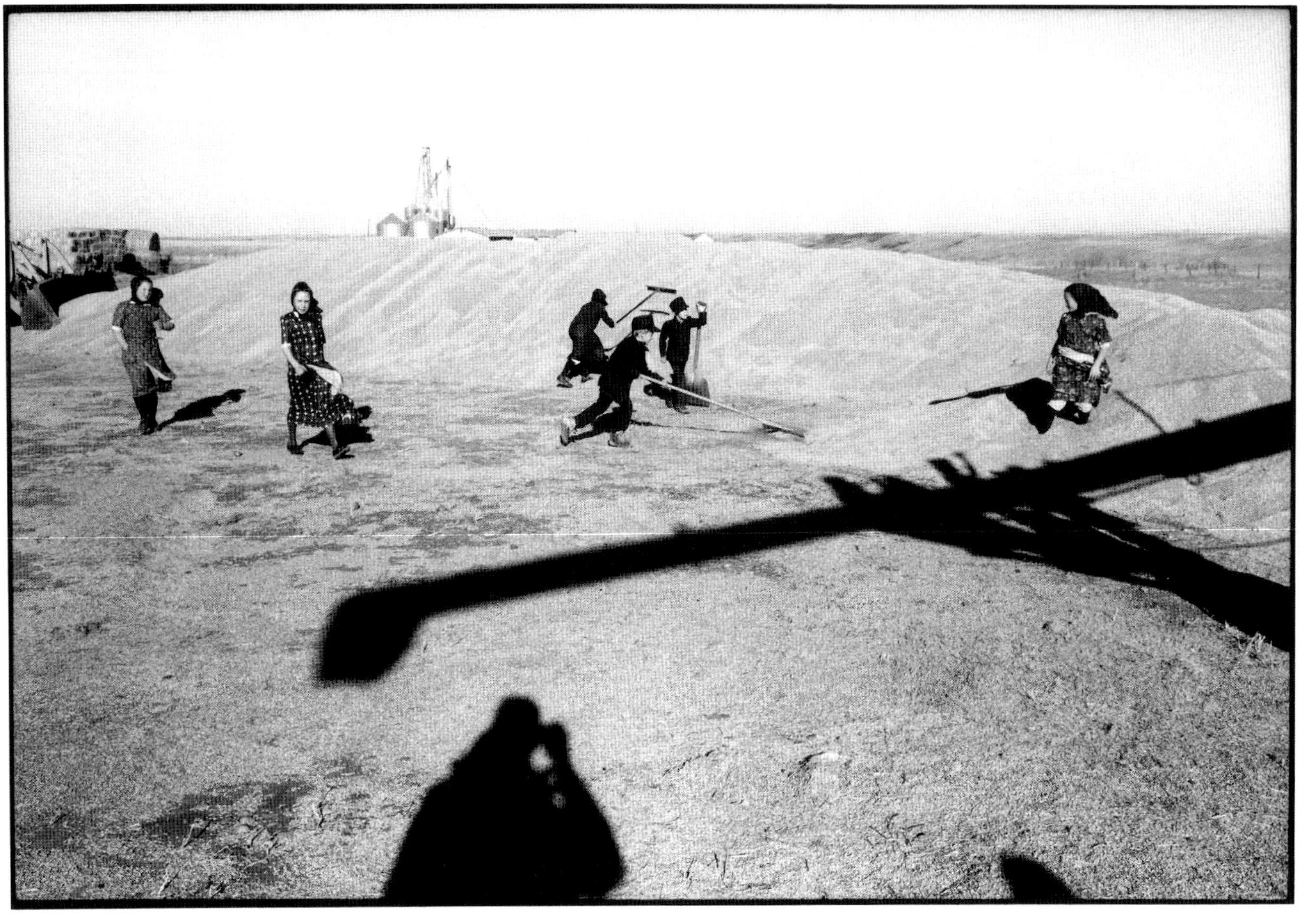

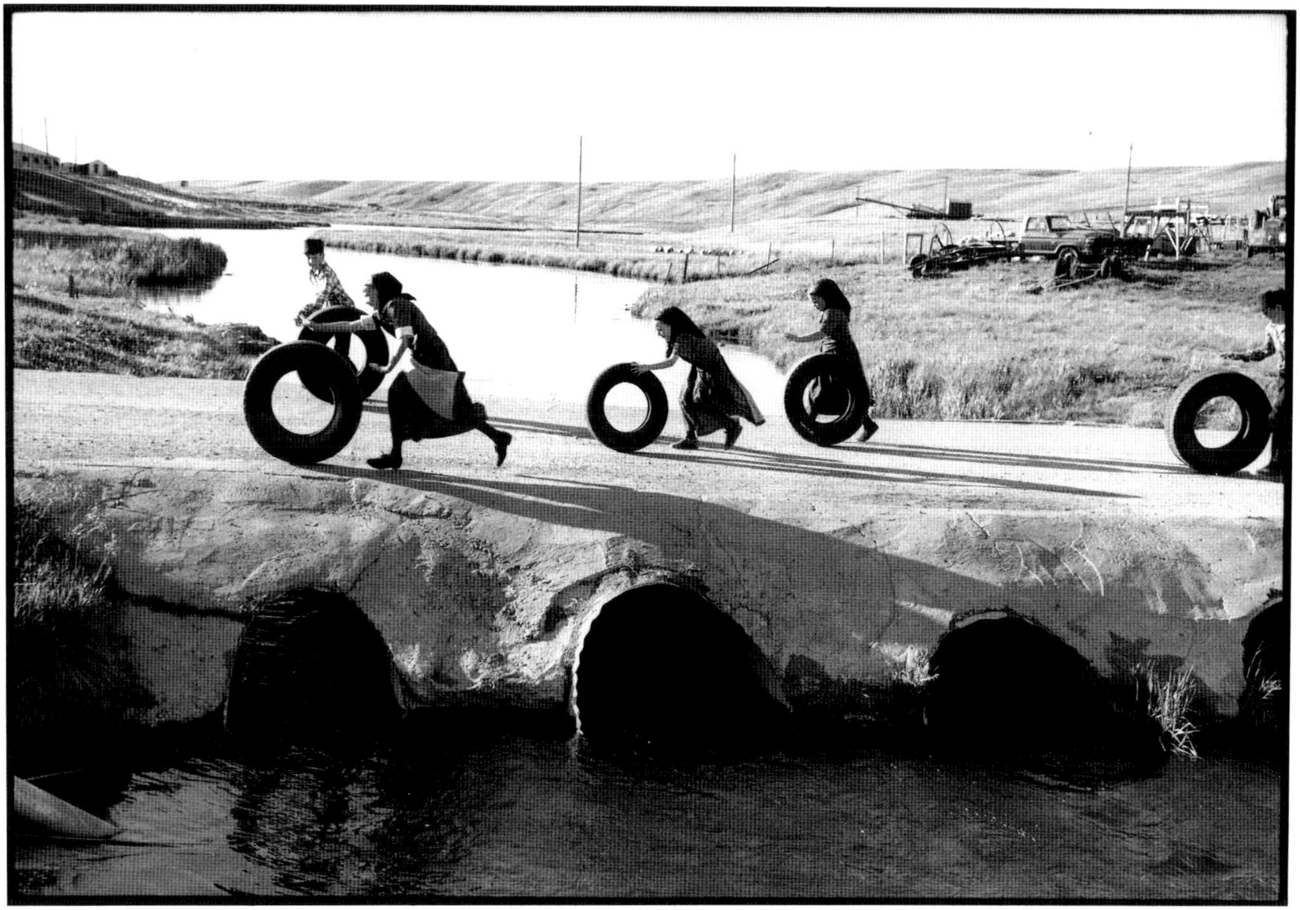

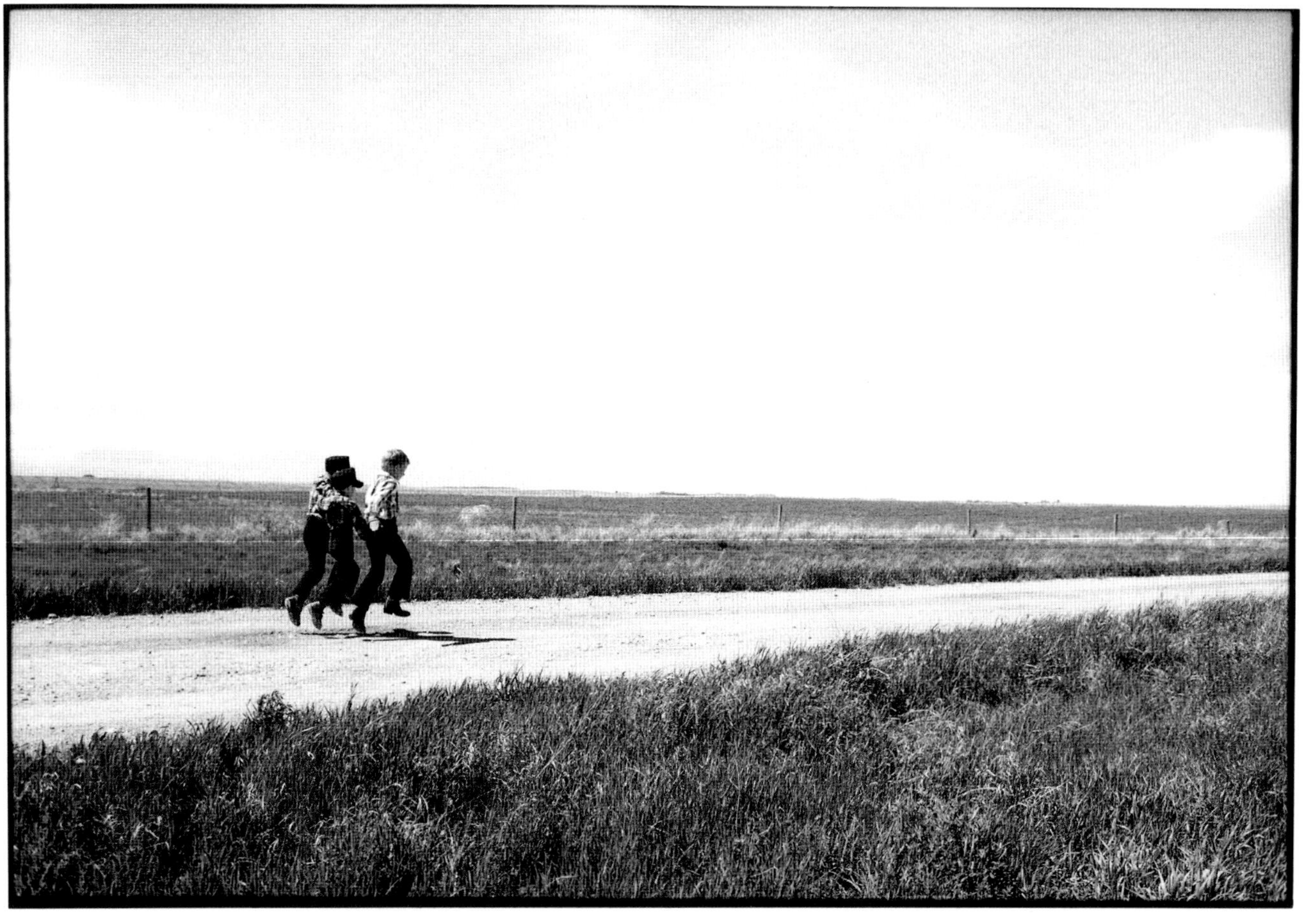

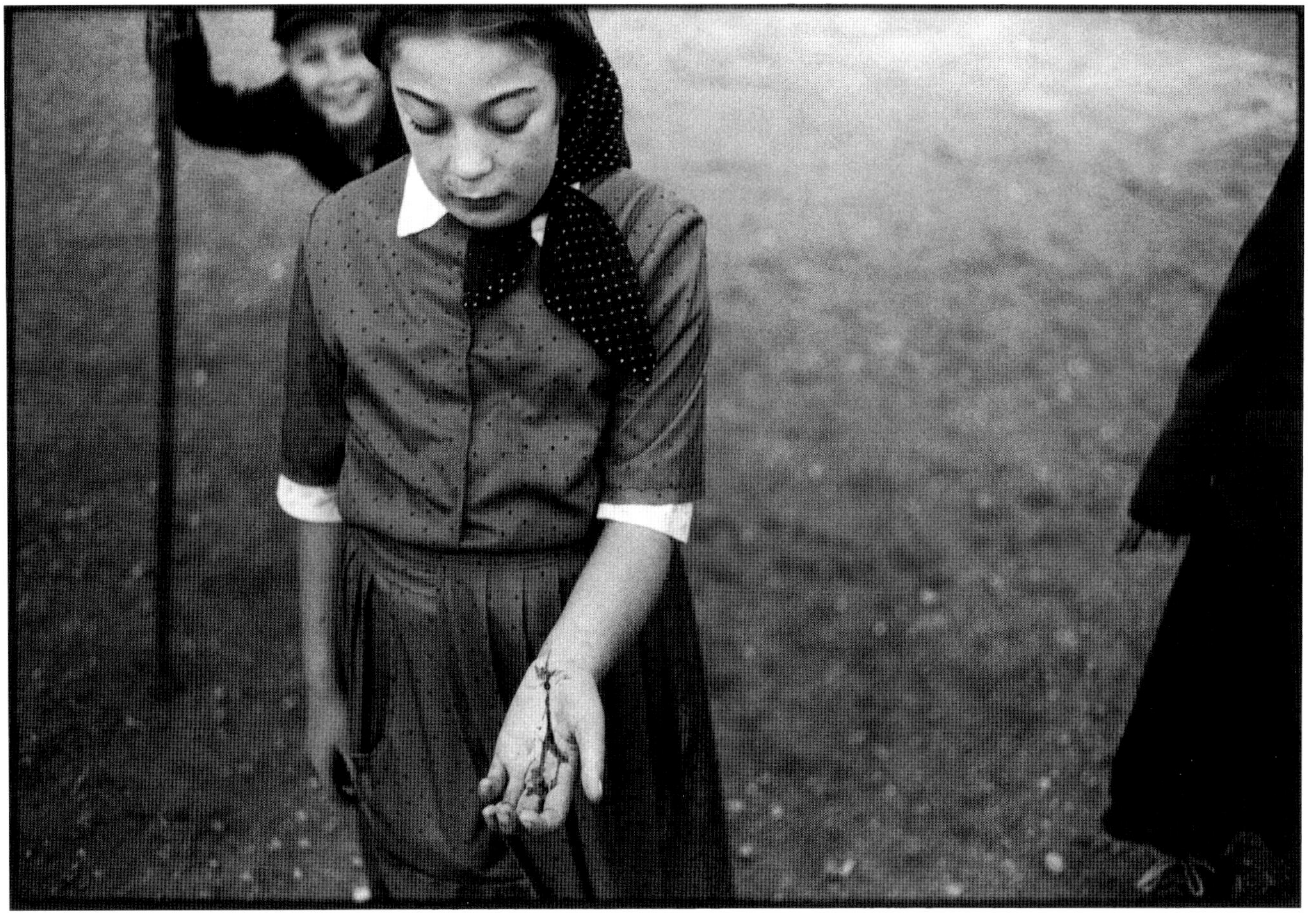

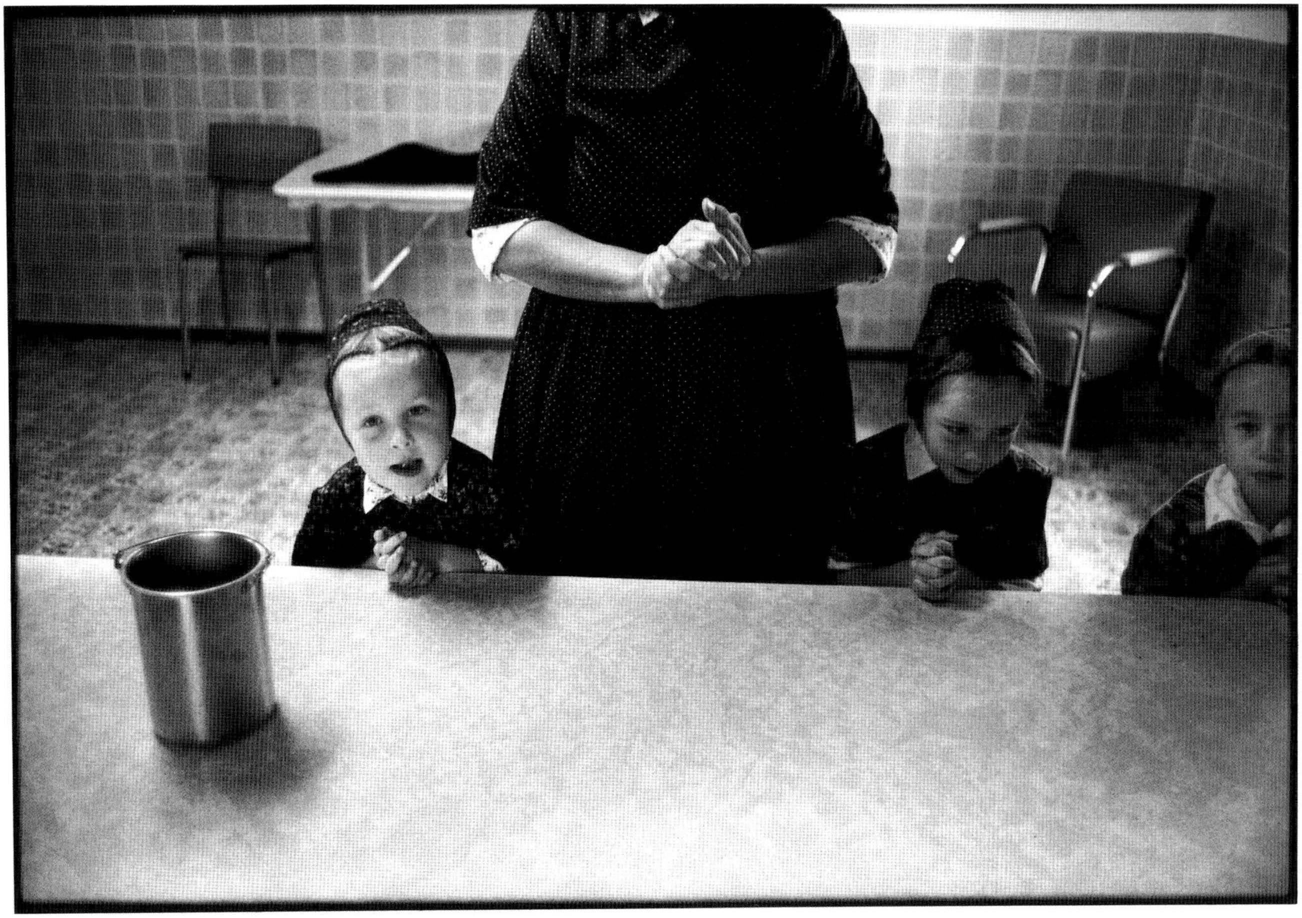

THE HOUSEHOLD OF FAITH

JUNE 4, 1999

I meet Rebecca Hofer, the widow of colony boss Mike, who died on February 16. They had married in January 1950 and moved to Little Bow Colony on January 15, 1983. She tells me she is suffering greatly from her husband's loss and that she has visited her husband's grave only once and found the experience so painful that she will not go again. We take some photographs of her with a group of her grandchildren. Later she tells me that her husband used to say, "Mom, it's time for bed," every night at 9:00. She wonders aloud how she is supposed to sleep now.

FEBRUARY 21, 2000

Death of a child: driving into the colony I see a muddy set of tracks through the snow leading to an excavated grave. Mathew comes up to the window of the truck dressed in his black Sunday clothes. "We are having a funeral today for Darren. He died yesterday. He was seven months old." I sit at the men's table in the crowded dining room. It is sombre and quiet. Across from us at the women's table, many are sitting with tears in their eyes. Later we attend the funeral service and file past the open coffin. The tiny child is propped up and looks like a perfect wax doll. He is buried surrounded by perhaps one hundred mourners in black. The dirt is swiftly shovelled over the little coffin, sounding like crashing surf. Later one of the men looks down, shaking his head in sorrow, and mutters, "That's another one we'll have to move." (Five coffins were eventually moved to the new colony site.)

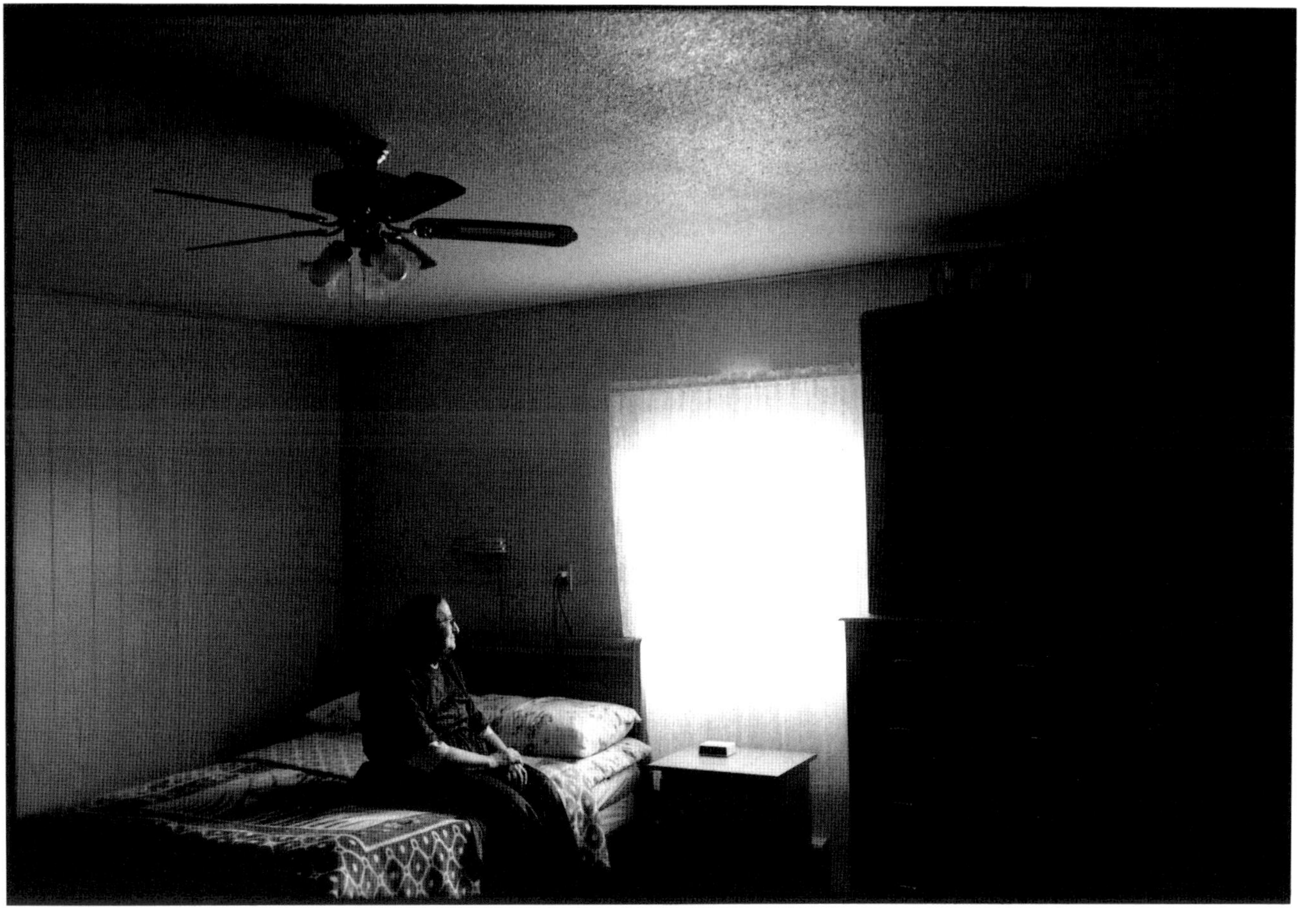

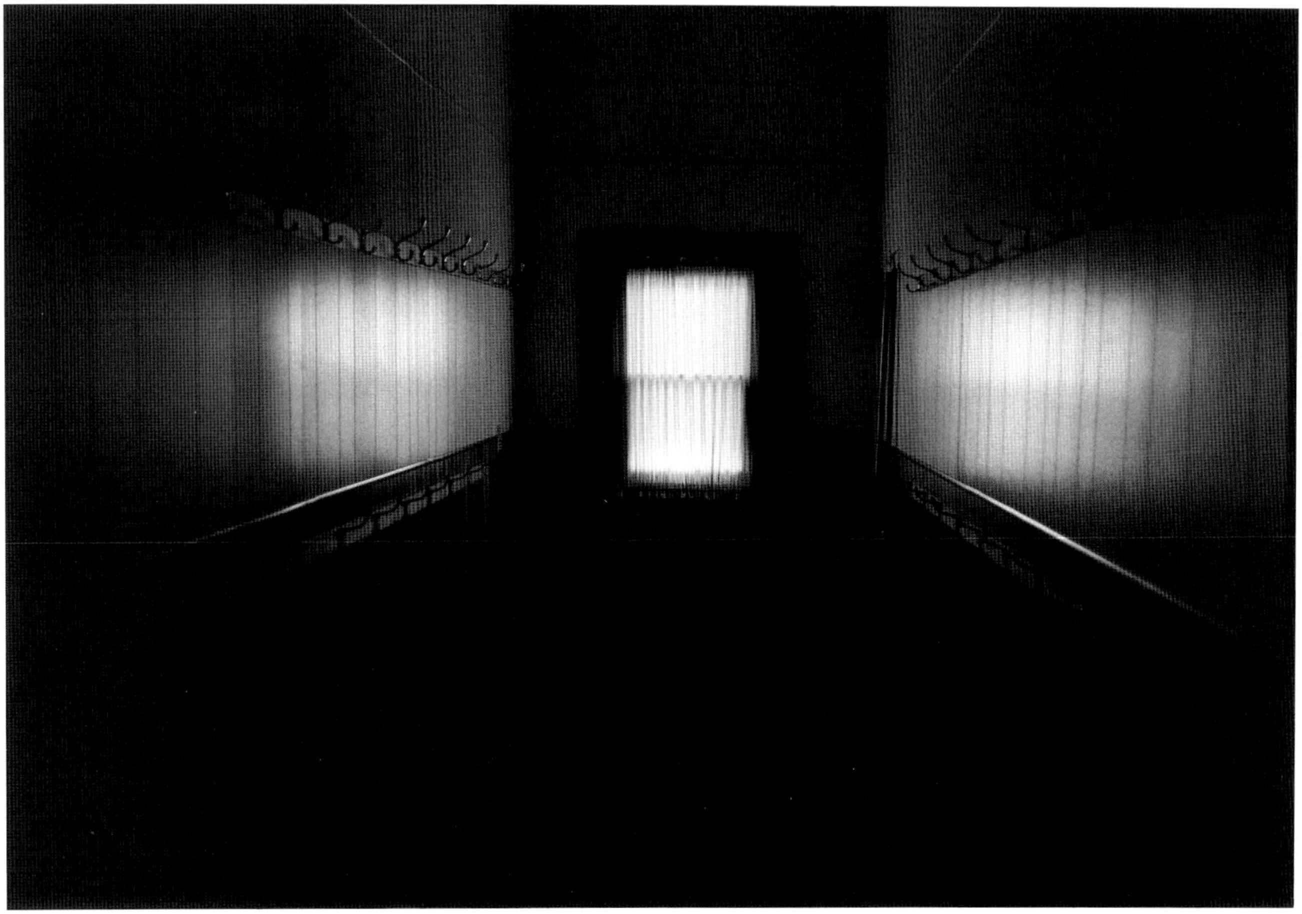

JUNE 13, 2000

News of the death of colony minister Darius. Drive with Mathew, listening to his Johnny Cash tape on the truck stereo, photographed preparation of grave site, photographed hogs being herded up for slaughter, went fishing with Mathew, helped unload the two-day-old ducks and geese that arrived that day.

Minister Darius's son tells me of his departed father. "He was big and strong but he never hurt nobody. He was born in May 1935. He was field boss for twenty-six years and minister for seventeen years."

Ruth, who takes care of the kindergarten, has to attend to some work for the funeral. She asks me to take charge of the kindergarten for a while. My charges—six little barefoot Hutterite girls aged three to five—are struck with glee at the thought of their indulgent "Uncle Garge" being in charge for a while. Lots of swinging, giggling, and running around ensues.

JULY 3, 2000

I bring a copy of Steve's photograph to his mother, Ruth. Steve has left the colony to work harvesting crops in the U.S. and his parents are saddened by his decision. Ruth gently cradles the print in her hands with moistening eyes and says, "This is like Steve walking in the door."

AUGUST 23, 2001

On our relationship with God, Minister Paul tells me: "He just wants us to thank him once in a while."

Katie tells me of attending the funeral of her uncle at the Gull Lake colony in Saskatchewan. He died at seventy-one. Three of his five children were mentally handicapped.

SEPTEMBER 3, 2001

Unseasonably warm and sunny day for the wedding of Tom and Lisa. A room in one of the houses on the colony is just *packed* with wedding gifts, which include bottles of bleach, lamps, ceiling fans, towel racks, and numerous clocks. During the wedding ceremony, Lisa stands slightly behind Tom, as is the custom, then gently presses into his back. After the wedding there is a meal and singing. This will be the last wedding performed at Little Bow Colony.

DECEMBER 26, 2001

That afternoon I have coffee with Pete. I mention an issue in my life that had been causing me some stress and worry and ask how he deals with things like that in his life. He catches my eye with a steady gaze and says, "George, there are two ways to believe in God. One is that you simply believe that he exists … the other way is that you believe that he will help you when you need him. You need to know and *believe* that he will help you."

AUGUST 24, 2002

Minister Paul Hofer shows me his new desk with approximately three hundred bound sermons and special prayers that he will deliver on occasions, including funerals for "the good ones and the bad ones too," he says with a wink.

Paul left the colony way of life behind when he was in his early twenties. After being away for six years, he began to re-examine his life. His mother asked him if he would return to the colony. With some reluctance he agreed. Not long after, he met Ruth, the woman who was eventually to become his wife. In 1979 Paul and Ruth, who was expecting their first child, Steve, were part of a small group sent to establish Little Bow Colony. With a little tilt of his head, Paul says, "George, we must place our faith in the good Lord. He will always watch over us."

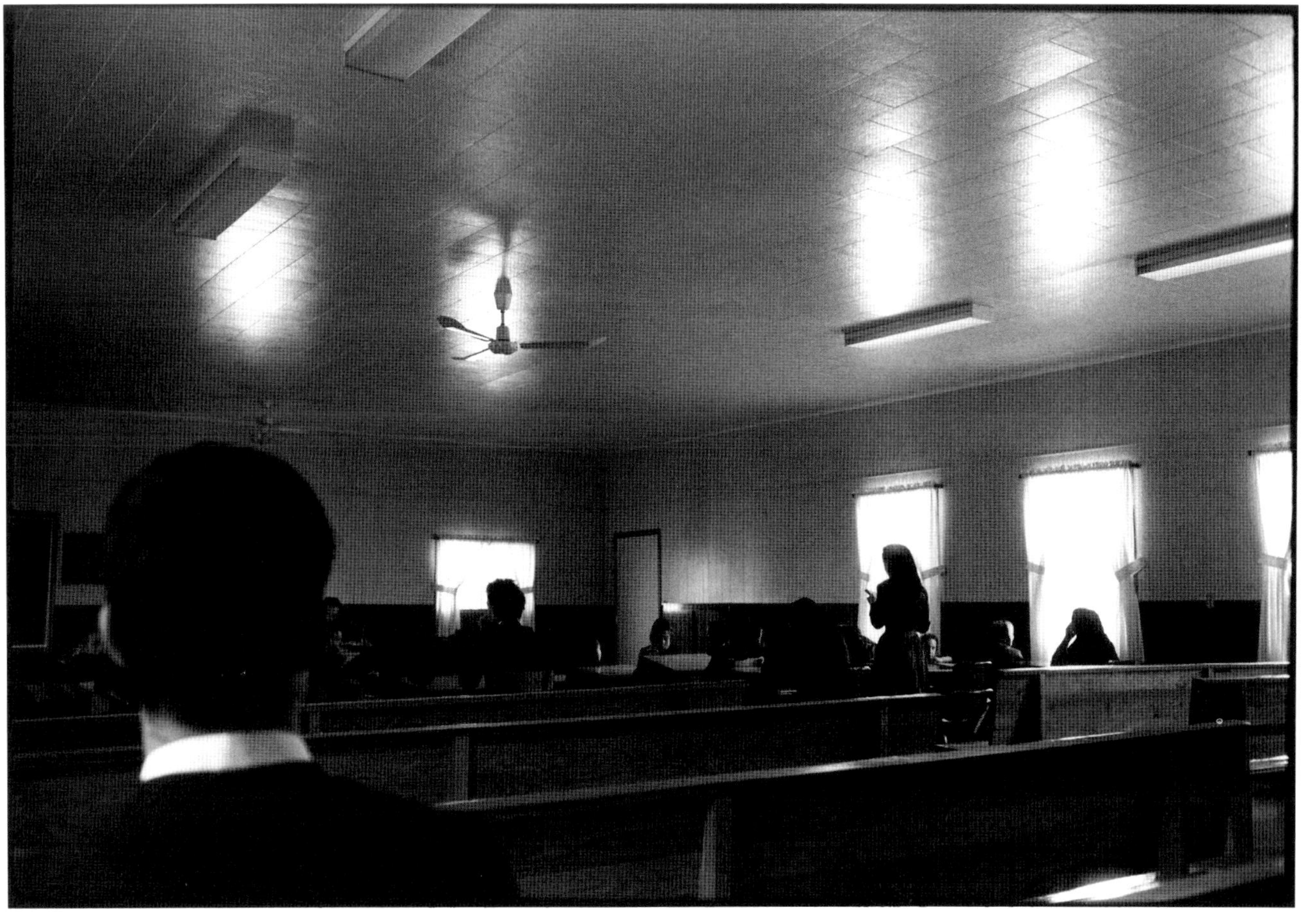

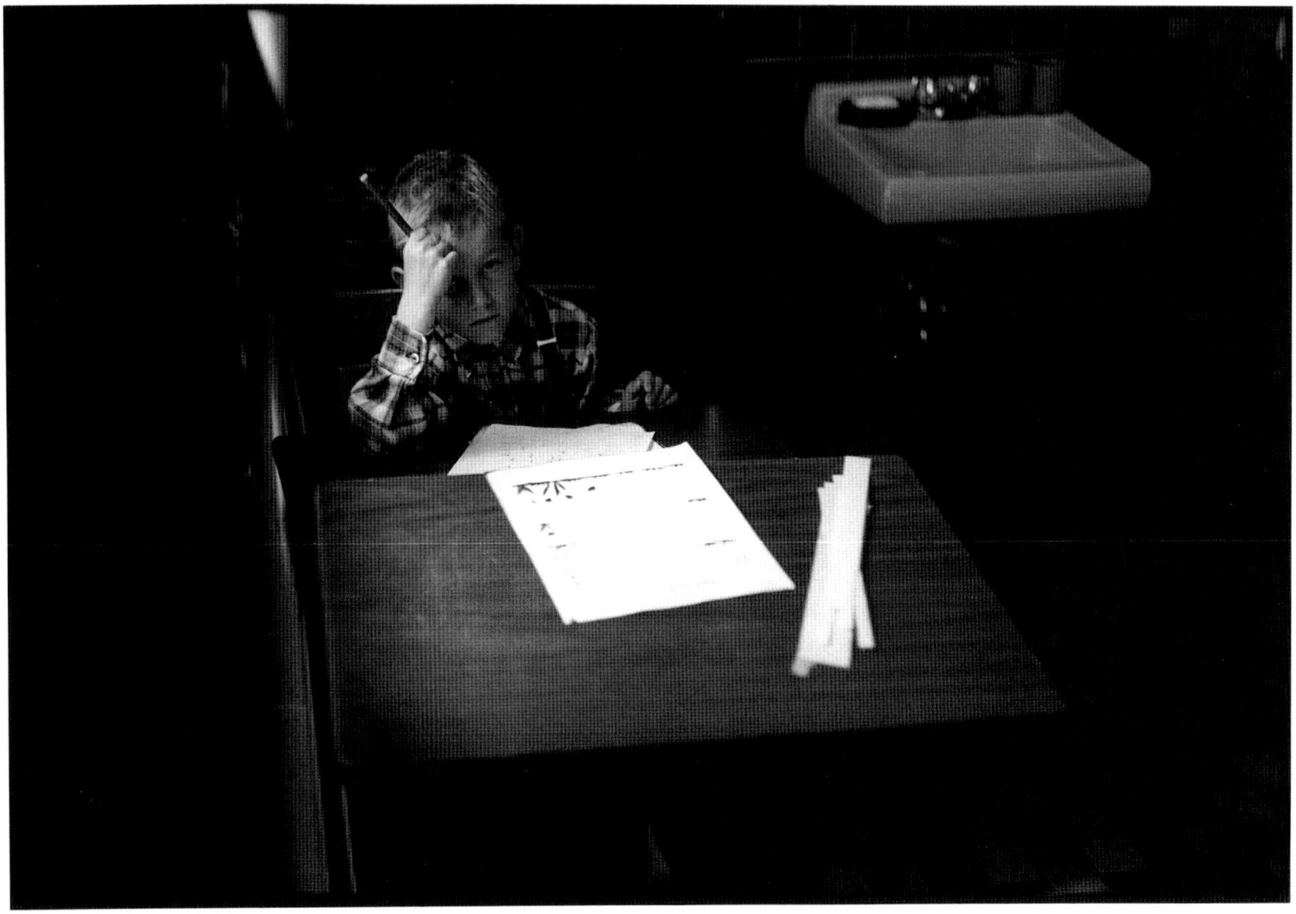

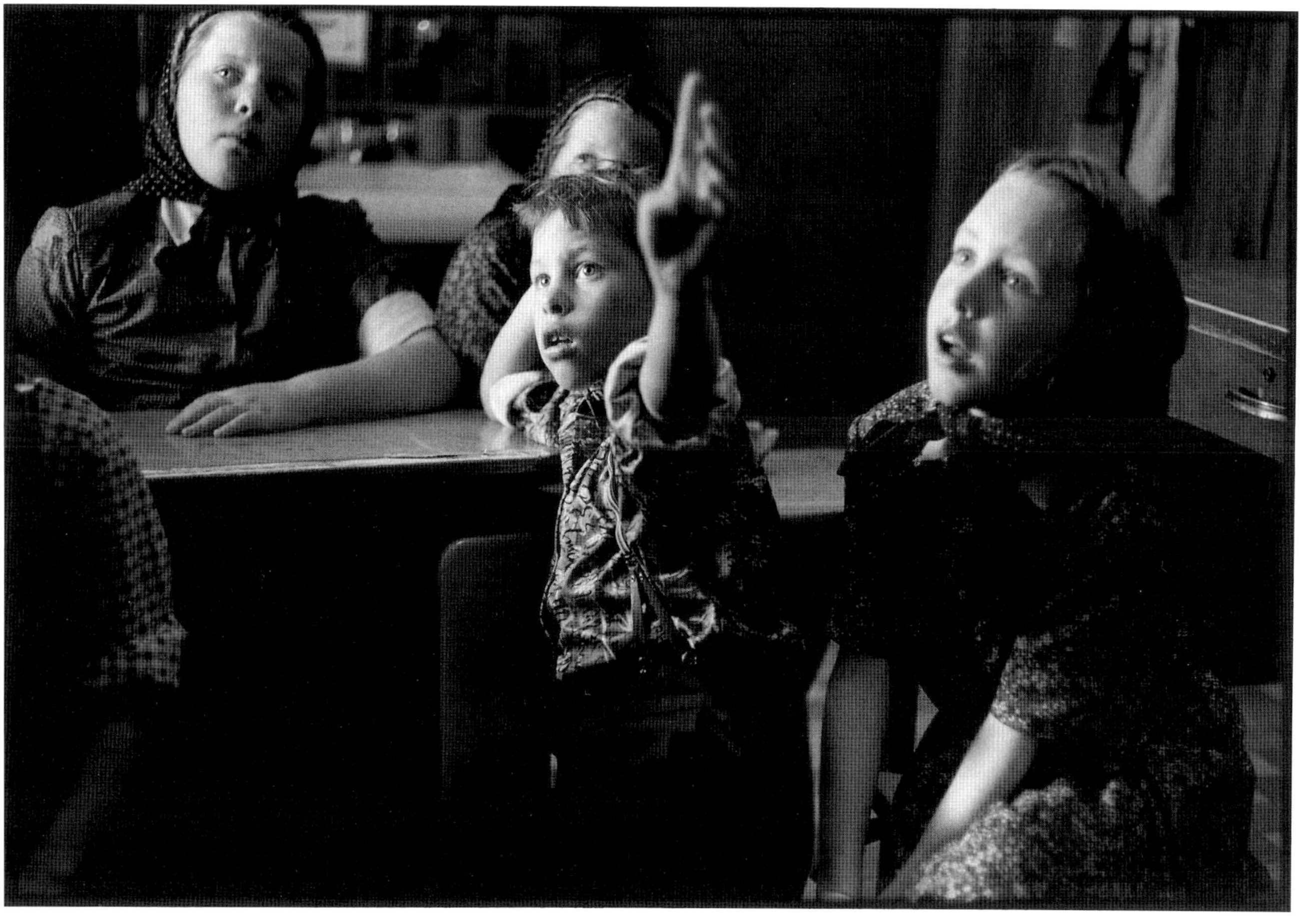

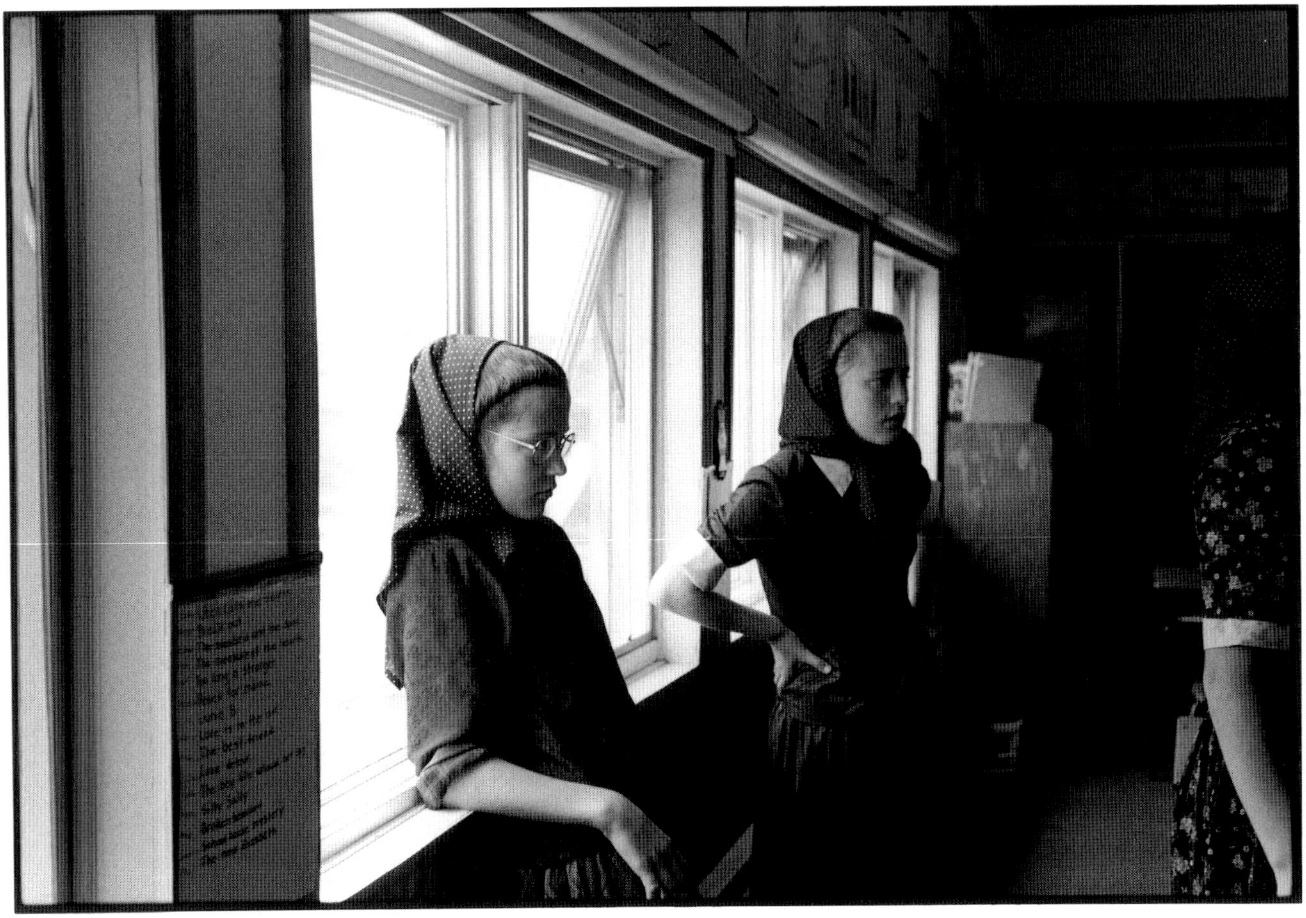

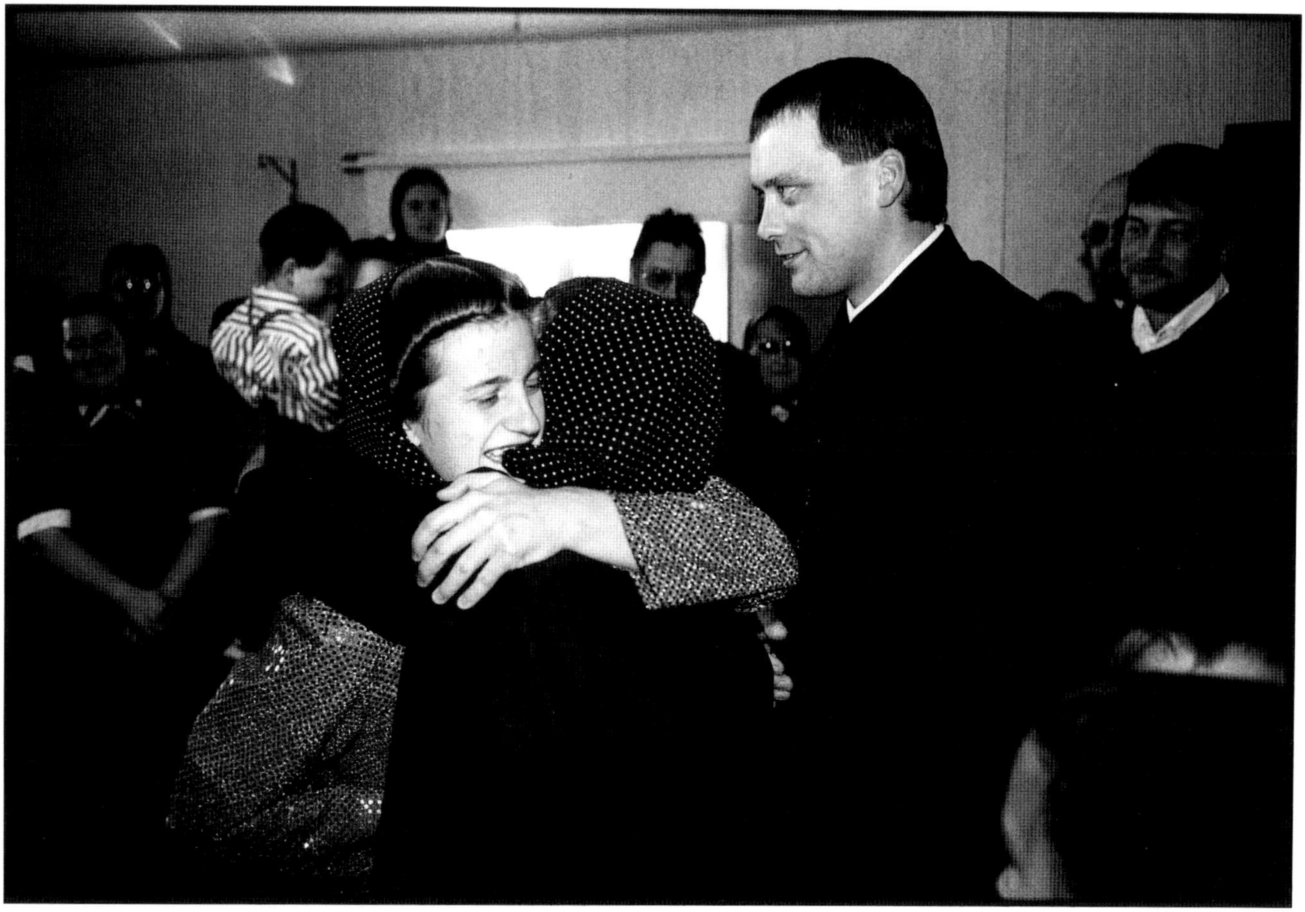

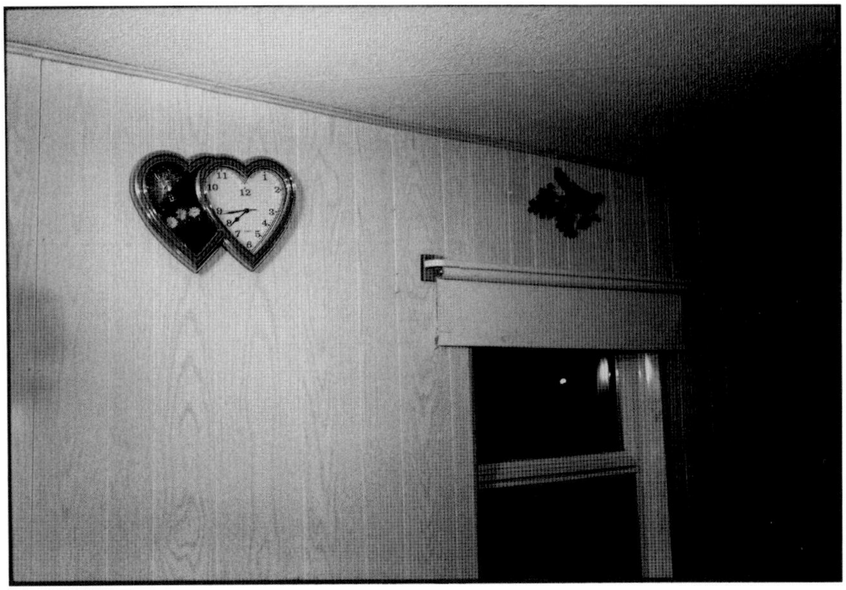

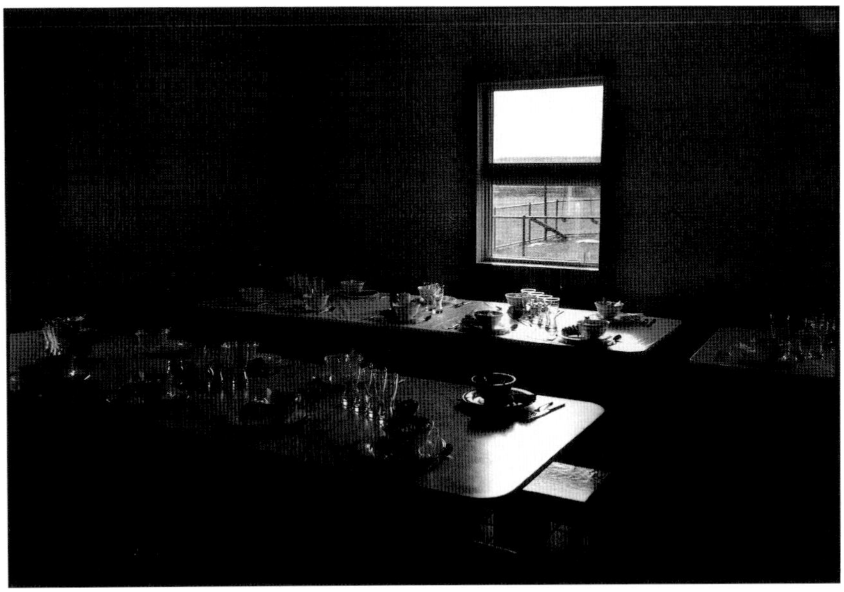

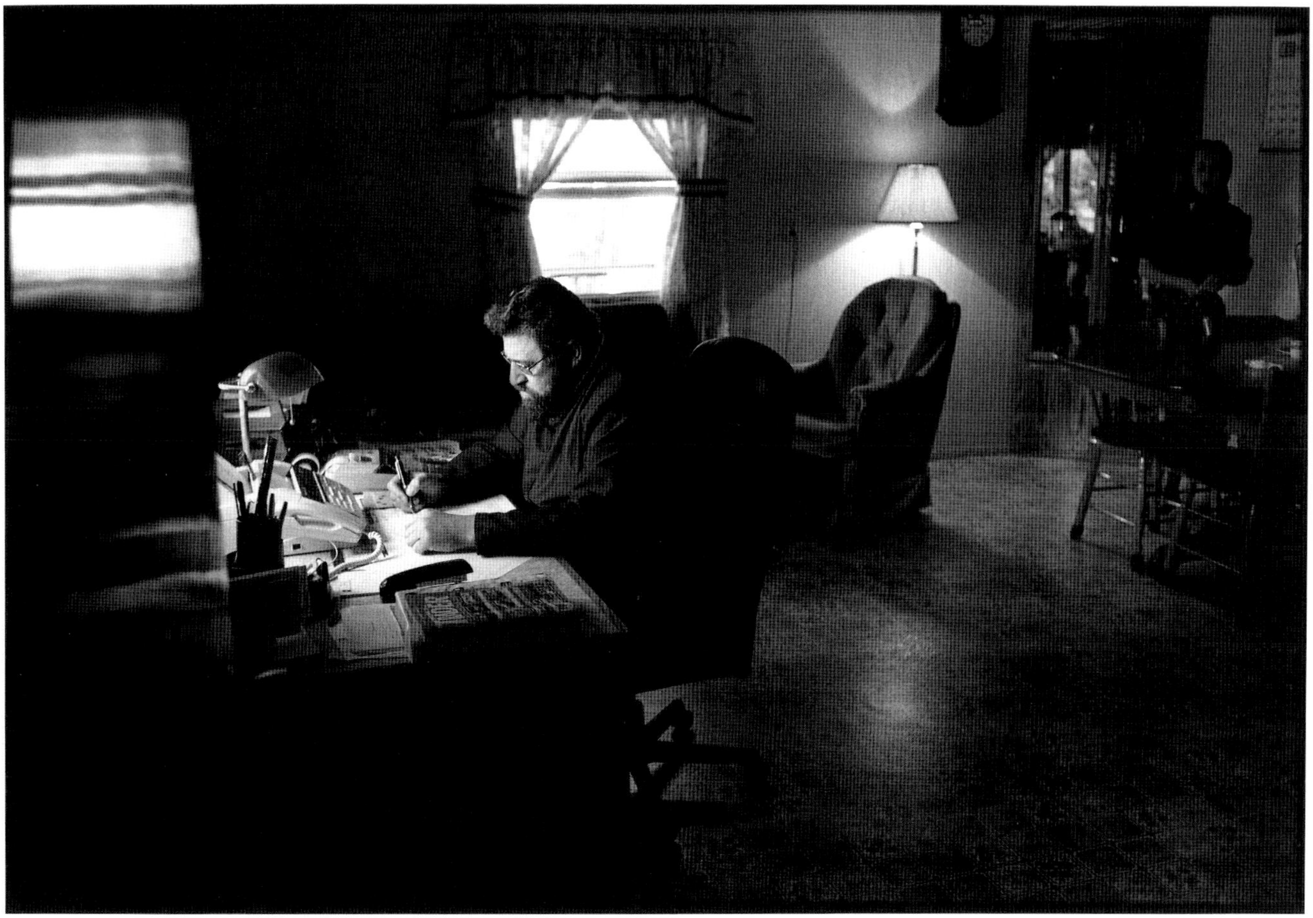

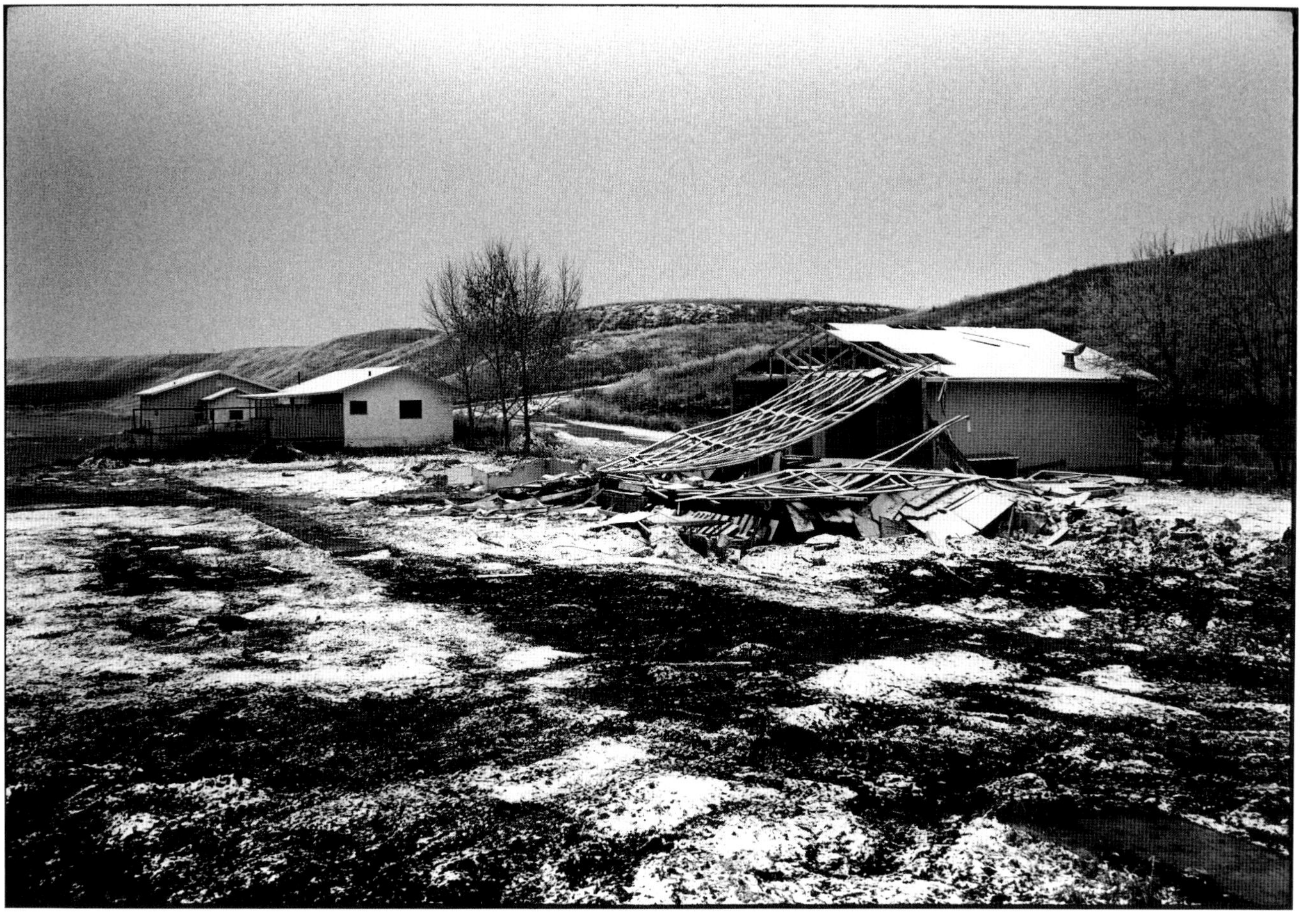

A NEW BEGINNING

APRIL 2002

Approximate population of Little Bow—April 2002—115 people.

APRIL 19, 2002

I return to the colony site after everyone has left. Cresting the hill, I drop down into the valley as I have done dozens of times over the past four years. The emptiness and stillness on that foggy morning are startling. I go into the church, into the school, into the children's dining room, into the slaughterhouse, and into the houses.

The central courtyard appears to have been stripped of grass. Closer inspection reveals that the grass has been worn off by the many vehicles that had been used to load up household effects. An enormous flock of birds circles, filling the grey sky with their song. By mid-afternoon many of the women and older girls arrive to pick up remaining household items. I drive four of them to the new colony and arrive just before school is out. Later the children take me for a walk to look at the wonderful new buildings, shops, and barns. They are happy and excited with the new place. The adults seem tired, but happy as well to finally be settling after so many years of uncertainty. Katie Hofer reminds me that the moving of the colony by a provincial government has never happened before. I have dinner with the children in their new dining room, attend church, and stop for a visit with Katie's husband, Pete. He shows me his new turquoise Macintosh computer. One of the colony women, Barbara, tells me how much pleasure the new colony site gives her. She had been brought up on an open prairie colony. When she was first married and came to the Little Bow valley, she felt hemmed in and cried for days. "I couldn't see far," she explains.

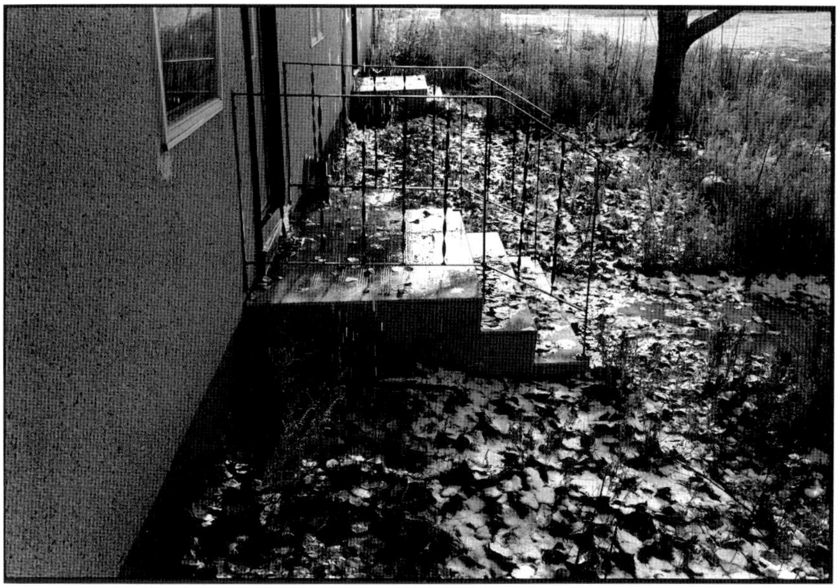

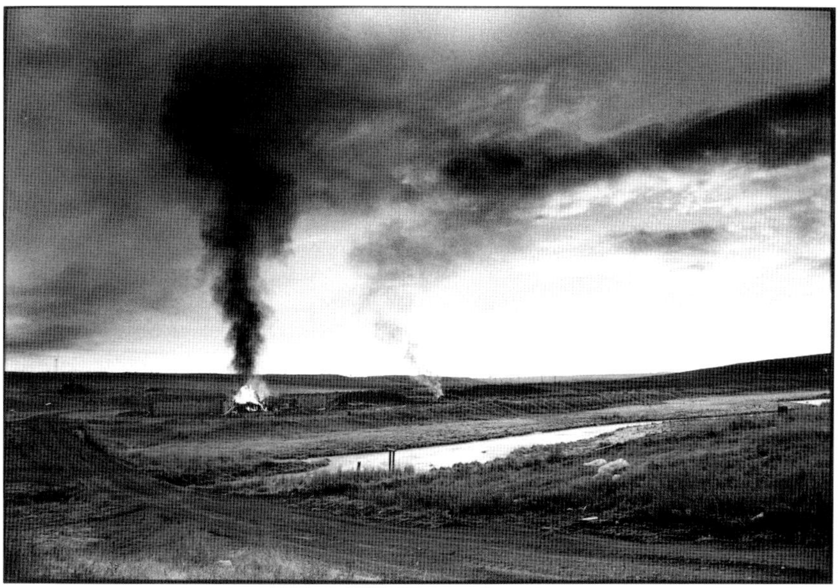

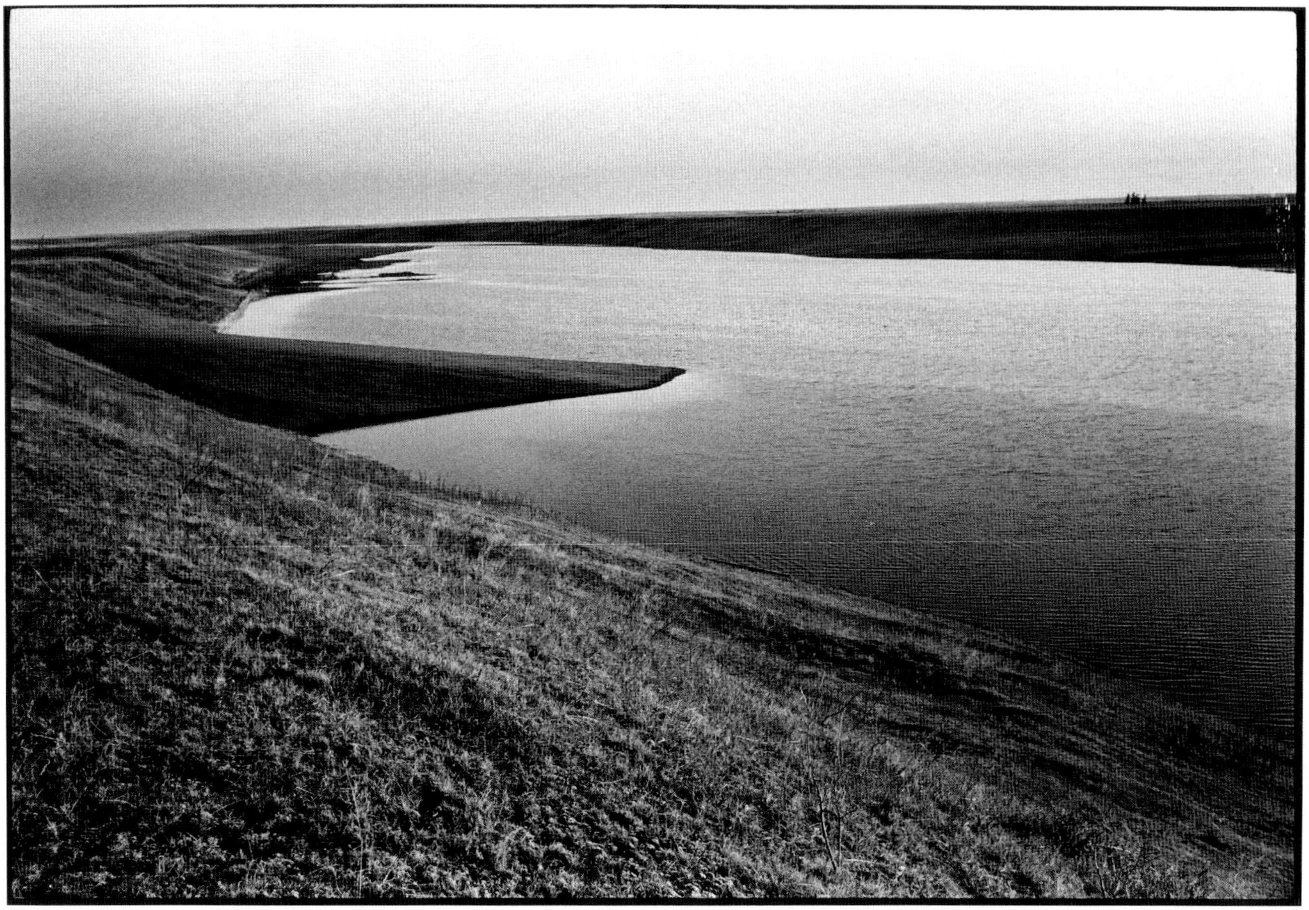

JUNE 15, 2002

A summer flood has submerged the bridge in the centre of the colony. The colony site is still and lush with overgrown vegetation. I hear a truck coming. It is Ed, the colony boss. He cautions me about the dangers of falling into the holes that remain after many of the trees were excavated. He asks me to take a few portraits of him sitting on the steps of his abandoned house. He looks into the central courtyard, his voice just above the level of a whisper. "It makes my heart burn to see the place like this. I'll be glad when everything is gone."

DECEMBER 18, 2002

Approaching the colony just before dawn in the pale half-light, I can see a thick, black mushroom cloud of smoke rising from the valley. I drive forward past a large orange sign with black lettering. It reads: "Permanent road closure will occur on Dec 2/02."

The dairy barn is engulfed in flame. Beyond that the corral has been pushed into a heap that has been transformed into a cone of flame. Everything else in the colony is gone. I feel strange, without bearings as I walk through the site. That evening I attend the children's Christmas concert at the new colony site. Dorothy proudly lifts her healthy, chubby baby girl for me to see. She describes the infant as a "miracle baby," explaining that she had been born eleven weeks premature and weighed just over three pounds. After the concert we all go for a meal of cheese and meat and buns.

APRIL 20, 2003 (EASTER SUNDAY)

I drive out early on Easter Sunday morning, looking down at the broad lake that covers the colony site. Looking southeast, I see a tiny rainbow.

ACKNOWLEDGEMENTS

This book is dedicated to my parents George and Del Webber. I also wish to acknowledge the special people who have sustained and inspired me over the years. Thanks to the people of Little Bow Colony; Eugene Atget; Mary, Jack, Ben, Ty, Trish, and Beth Baines; Donna Balzer; Rusty Bragg; Ron Burton; David Campion and Sandra Shields; Henri Cartier-Bresson; Sister Helen Claire; Chris Clarke; Father Pat Cramer; Bruce Davidson; Don Denton; Peter and Beth Duthie; William Eggleston; Walker Evans; David Fahie; Robert Frank; Pat Furneaux; Mary Pat Gibson; Elizabeth Giles; Jennifer Herzog; Betty Hessel; Father Jacques Johnson; Todd Korol; Patricia, Roger, Joseph, George, Thomas, and William Lace; Chee Lau; Gwyn Llewelyn; Alison MacCallum; Betty, Phil, Joel, and Nicole Michaud; Father Bob Mitchell; Kit Munro; Joan Newman; Harry Palmer; Vince Pietropaolo; Craig Richards; Orest Semchishen; Stephen Shore; Brock Silversides; Don, Laurelle, Chandler, Brienne, and Parker Tully; Tim Van Horn and Kris Wagner; Bill Webber; Jim and Chris Webber; Marge Webber; and Ken Young.

ABOUT THE AUTHOR

Award-winning documentary photographer George Webber has devoted much of his life to capturing images of the vast Canadian prairie landscape and the lives of the people who call it home. Born in Drumheller, Alberta, in 1952, Webber began his career in photography after graduating from Carleton University's School of Journalism in 1974. Since then, he has taken thousands of powerful, evocative, mostly black-and-white photographs that reveal his fascination and affection for the people, towns, and landscape of the Canadian West. For Webber, it is the memories attached to these images that define his work. Webber's photographs are included in museum collections the world over and have been published in numerous prestigious books and magazines. Webber's awards include the Ford of Canada Photographic Grand Prix in 1992 and the Silver Award in photojournalism at the 2002 National Magazine Awards for his photo essay *People of the Blood*, shot on the Blood reserve of Southern Alberta south of Calgary. In 1999 Webber was recognized for his achievements with his induction into the Royal Canadian Academy of Arts—the oldest bilingual visual arts organization in Canada.

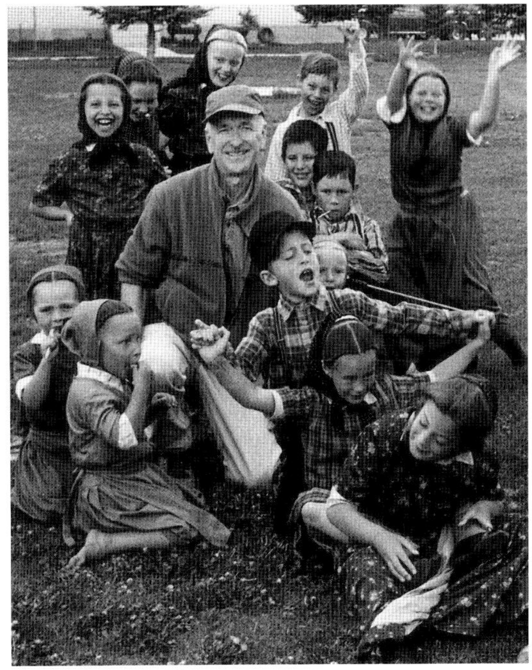

Photo: Mathew Hofer

George Webber lives in Calgary, where he works as a freelance photographer. He also teaches photography at the Southern Alberta Institute of Technology.

ABOUT THE PHOTOGRAPHS

Note: page numbers listed in brackets.

[13] Swallows fill the sky along the sinewy Little Bow River, downstream from the colony.

[15] Sharon Hofer (left) and Marilyn Hofer (right) standing above the colony under dark storm clouds

[17 bottom] Mathew Hofer fishing in the tranquil Little Bow River near the colony

[18] Children's footprints in the snow on the frozen Little Bow River, downstream from the colony

[19] Children walking out along the frozen Little Bow River to greet me

[21] Julie Hofer (left) twists little Brenda Hofer's head towards the camera. "Look at Garge," she coos, as Joel Hofer stands in the background and Maria Hofer moves out of the right side of the picture.

[22] As I bend down to take a picture, one of the young girls snatches my cap and places it on Wendy Hofer's head. I am rewarded with a gleeful, gap-toothed smile.

[23] Maria Hofer with her blonde hair in a tangle under her bonnet

[25 top] One of the older girls unbraids Maria Hofer's hair before the Saturday washing and braiding.

[25 bottom] Miriam Hofer washes Julie Hofer's hair.

[26 top] Sara Hofer braids her daughter Maria's hair at their kitchen table.

[26 bottom] One of the elder women of the colony affixes Maria's bonnet after her hair has been braided.

[27] Miriam Hofer (left) and Clara Hofer (right) prepare to sweep the floor in the children's dining room after lunch

[28] Clara Hofer (left), Joanne Hofer (centre), and Grandma Katie Hofer (right) prepare to make buns. A fresh bundle of buns are brought to the school every Friday morning for the teachers.

[30] A visitor from another colony (left), Martha Hofer (centre), and Ruth Ann Hofer (right) prepare to make buns as the children look on.

[31] Miriam Hofer holds Julie Hofer as Julie's mother, Katie, drives the tractor into the garden where they will all pick vegetables for market.

[32 top] Curtis Hofer smiling at me through a window, as the reflection of me holding my camera falls over his face

[32 bottom] Eddie Hofer (left), Mathew Hofer (centre), and Jason Hofer (right) walking along a gravel road near the colony, with my shadow in the foreground

[33] Sharon Hofer in the calf barn

[34] Sharon Hofer (foreground), Jamie Hofer (left), Timmy Hofer (right), and Maria Hofer (in the background) at the duck pen

[35] Pete Hofer, cow boss, in the dairy barn

[36 top] Timmy Hofer (foreground), Joel Hofer (left background), Martin Hofer (centre background), and Joey Hofer (right background) in the calf barn

[36 bottom] Thomas Hofer (left) and Mathew Hofer (right), with their border collie pup, Sampson

[37] Mathew Hofer with grain stalks

[38] Joey Hofer (left) and Maria Hofer (right) in the automotive shop

[39] Walking after evening meal on the road above the colony

[41] Clothesline

[42 top] Jonti Hofer, poultry man, sorting eggs

[42 bottom] A duck is lifted up into the light as Mathew Hofer looks on.

[43] Kathrine Hofer (standing on fence post), Arnie Hofer (with foot on fence), and Laura Hofer (standing on fence) at the duck and geese pen

[44] Miriam J. Hofer cutting a swath through the duck pen

[45] Laura Hofer (left), Marilyn Hofer (centre), Tabby Hofer (right), and Sara Hofer (far right) herding geese into their pen

[47] Paul Hofer (centre) and other young men preparing to butcher turkeys

[48 top] Jonti Hofer (foreground) supervising the slaughter of the geese

[48 bottom] Geese being bled out on rack create a circle of blood on the ground.

[49 top] Ruth Ann Hofer working on the poultry-processing line

[49 bottom] Annie Hofer removing pin feathers from poultry

[50] Sharon Hofer walking after the sheep

[51] Boys and sheepdog, with sheep

[53 top] Shearing sheep

[53 bottom] Shearing sheep

[54 top] Shearing sheep

[54 bottom] Packing the wool

[55 top] Bedroom wall of Mathew Hofer, featuring his truck poster, pig poster, and key chain collection

[55 bottom] Mathew Hofer administering antibiotics to a pig

[56] Mathew Hofer tending to hogs before slaughter

[57] Butchering hogs on a misty winter morning

[58] Paul Hofer (left) carving out blocks of ice to free the water pump

[59] Annie Hofer picking beans in the garden

[60 top] Esther Hofer (standing), Katie Hofer (bending left), and Julie Hofer (right) harvesting cabbage

[60 bottom] Pete Hofer washing freshly harvested potatoes

[61] Boys tending geese

[62] Melissa Hofer (left) and Debbie Hofer (right) after harvesting potatoes

[63] Susie Hofer (left), Pete Hofer (centre), and Katie Hofer (right) packing vegetables for market

[64] Susie Hofer (left), Katie Hofer (centre), and Sara Hofer (right) in the poppy field

[65] Miriam Hofer (foreground) and Abigail Hofer (background) doing crabapple preserves

[66] Jason Hofer (left), Mathew Hofer (centre), and Curtis Hofer (right) watching the combine

[67 top] Gary Hofer at the grain bin

[67 bottom] Mathew Hofer during fence mending

[68] Curtis Hofer (left) and Thomas Hofer (right) during fence mending

[69 top] Arnie Hofer in the calf barn

[69 bottom] Interior of the dairy barn

[71] Children playing in the field

[72] Laura Hofer (left, looking at camera), Marilyn Hofer (centre), and Joel Hofer (background) playing on the clotheslines

[73 top] Skating on the Little Bow River

[73 bottom] Children jumping onto the frozen Little Bow River

[74] Hockey on the frozen sewage pond

[77] Children tobogganing at lunch break

[78] Children tobogganing at lunch break

[79] Mothers tobogganing after children have returned to schoolroom. Left to right: Annie Hofer, Joanne Hofer, Kathie Hofer, and Katie Hofer

[80 top] Sharon Hofer (left), Marilyn Hofer (centre), and Eddie Hofer (right) using the poultry slaughter rack as a merry-go-round

[80 bottom] Laura Hofer and other children running uphill into shadows

[81 top] Mathew Hofer (left), Eddie Hofer (right), and Paul Hofer (background) leaning back into a powerful wind above the Little Bow River

[81 bottom] Girls with aprons blown up by powerful wind

[82 top] Jamie Hofer in the Little Bow River

[82 bottom] Mathew Hofer floating on an inner tube on the Little Bow River

[83] Julie Hofer jumping off the diving board into the Little Bow River

[84 top] Boys playing on the harrowing machinery

[84 bottom] Boys playing on the hay bales

[85] Kathrine Hofer jumping into the wheat pile

[86] Children playing near shadow of grain auger

[87] Sammy Hofer (left), Kathrine Hofer (centre), Tabby Hofer (right), and Debbie Hofer (far right) rolling tires into playground for end-of-school-year sports day

[88] Jamie Hofer (left), Joey Hofer (centre), and Martin Hofer (right) skipping along the road above the colony

[89] Laura Hofer shows her cut hand after taking a fall. Simon Hofer looks over her shoulder.

[91] Saying grace at kindergarten

[93] Widow Rebecca Hofer in her bedroom

[94] Church hallway with coat hooks

[97] German school lesson

[98] Timmy Hofer, grade one student

[99] Melissa Hofer (left), Joel Hofer (centre), and Tabby Hofer (right) in English school at Little Bow Colony

[100] Miriam Hofer (left) and Clara Hofer (right) in English school at Little Bow Colony

[101] Lisa and Tom Hofer on their wedding day

[102 top] Clock on wedding day

[102 bottom] Tables set up for Tom and Lisa Hofer's wedding meal

[103] Colony boss Ed Hofer at his desk

[105] Demolition of the Little Bow Hutterite Colony

[107 top] Abandoned house during demolition of the colony

[107 bottom] Burning of the dairy barn during demolition of the colony

[108] Flooded colony site, Easter Sunday 2003

[111] George Webber with children, photo by Mathew Hofer

TECHNICAL NOTE

Camera: Leica M6
Lenses: 35mm + 50mm
Film: Ilford HP5
Reproduction prints: Ilford Multigrade RC
Exhibition prints: Ilford Multigrade FB

All film and prints were hand developed by the photographer.

ABOUT FIFTH HOUSE

Fifth House Publishers, a Fitzhenry & Whiteside company, is a proudly western-Canadian press. Our publishing specialty is non-fiction as we believe that every community must possess a positive understanding of its worth and place if it is to remain vital and progressive. Fifth House is committed to "bringing the West to the rest" by publishing approximately twenty books a year about the land and people who make this region unique. Our books are selected for their interest to readers, quality, saleability, and contribution to the understanding of western-Canadian (and Canadian) history, culture, and environment.